Post-Traumatic Streets Disorder:

A Battle Within

Written by **Justin "JD" Reeves**

Edited by: **Matt Machin**

Post traumatic streets disorder A battle within

To my best friend, my brother, Tony. First, I wanna say Rest In Paradise! Not a day goes by that I don't miss you. Sometimes I blame myself I wasn't there for you to help you fight those demons. I hate you cut your life short. It was still so much we had to accomplish. We were supposed to be here celebrating the release of this book together. You stayed up on me to make sure I was getting Everything done, every chance you got you told me you were proud of me and couldn't wait to read this book. So, this is my bittersweet symphony. I write and live with you in my heart and spirit, and I love you, brother.

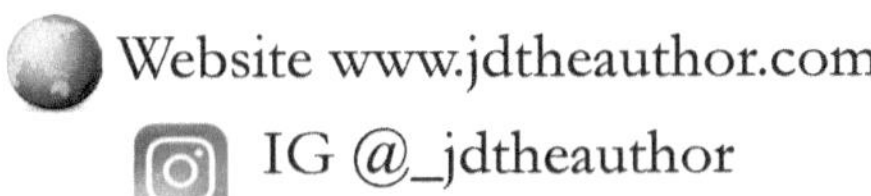

Website www.jdtheauthor.com

IG @_jdtheauthor

Contents

Introduction

I want to start by thanking God. I'm nothing without Him. God is the one that gave me the strength to persevere and survive through my struggles. He is the one reason I was truly never alone. I'm dedicating this book to my kids: Josiah, Justin, Justice, Eriyanna, and Ramella. Y'all don't know how many times y'all saved me from myself. Y'all introduced me to unconditional love. You love me through my imperfections and my shortcomings. For that, I will lay my life down to make sure y'all are good. Everything I'm doing is for y'all. I want y'all to see anything is possible, and you can do whatever you want to do in life. Just don't give up.

I want to thank my editor, Matt Machin. This book wouldn't be what it is without you. You really helped me dig deeper. You pushed me, and that was exactly what I needed. This is one of many masterpieces we are going to work on together, my friend.

To my business and life coach, Lance Knaub: I want to thank you and your company, Denali Consulting. You couldn't have come in my life at a better moment to help me reach levels I used to only dream about. Being around you in this short amount of time has helped me level up, and I'm looking forward to working with you in the future. Everyone should go purchase and read Lance's book after this one. It's called *The 4% Break-Thru.*

I want to give a special thanks to both of my mothers, my birth mom and my adopted mom. To my birth mom: even though I never got to meet you, none of this would be possible if you didn't carry me in your belly. So, regardless of choices you made or the life you were dealt, I thank you for that gift of life, alone. To my adopted mother, Elva: Even though our relationship was rocky through the years, you're still the only mother I know, and you tried, to the best of your ability, despite all I put you through. Most of the time, I'll admit, it was me. I wouldn't let you in; I kept you at a distance no one could reach, and I will love you forever.

I want to thank my best friend, my brother Latrell. You have been down with me since day one, and you've always been one phone call away. Even though I drive you crazy with my ideas, you have always been there and believed in me, but here you are reading my book, bro. It was all worth it. You are the true definition of a mud brother (as opposed to a blood brother), because we got out of the mud together.

To my bro Bubba: Even though we don't always see eye-to-eye, I know you are always in my corner. We've been through so much together and always held each other accountable. You've always been a standup guy and never folded on me. Watching the man and father you have become has been an inspiration. You are another individual who never let their situation define them. Look at you now; so many people counted you out and thought you was a lost cause and would throw your life away. You're proving them wrong, something I knew you could do.

My bro De in Colorado: you're another one that has always been one phone call away when I needed you.

Mama Jada, I thank you for being a mother figure in my life and always being there when I needed to talk. Even holding me accountable at times—that was well-needed. To my boy Ny Naphtali: We met at the bottom in Flatbush. I was at one of my lowest points at one time, and every day, you gave me words of inspiration and made sure I was good, and I'm thankful to you. Blessings to you, your queen, and little kings. To the one I call Unc: Windell, I met you when I was fourteen, and you took me under your wing, gave me knowledge of self, and was there every time I needed you. To be honest, you are the person who showed me what a man is and how a man is supposed to take care of his family. To my grandmother Pauline, who never once brought up the fact I was adopted and loved me like one of her flesh-and-blood grandsons. You were there to always put a positive bug in my ear, and I'll never forget that. I will forever miss your guidance. Rest In Paradise.

I want to thank my cousin Kevin, who was the first person to show me what a hustler is and what a hustle was. When I was young and you used to take me with you, you probably thought I was a kid and wasn't paying attention. Nah, I was taking notes on how fly you were. How fly your car was, and the big knots in your pockets. People can guess about the life of a hustler; they can listen to it in a rap song or watch it on TV, but to live the life of a hustler is another thing entirely. I wanted to be like my cousin Kevin.

I want to give a special thank-you to my mentor, who became my big brother, Michael Breedlove. Man, I can write a page about you alone and the things you've done for me without asking for anything back. You have been an angel in my life, for real, bro. You introduced me to your family, and they immediately took me in as one of the tribe, and I love you forever for that, bro. As you'll all learn in the rest of this book, I had trouble with the whole family thing when I was starting out. I want to thank my boy, M.O. at V12 studios. Back in 2015 when I had nothing, you gave me an opportunity when no one else was giving them out, and you showed me how to take nothing and turn it into something. You had just started V12, and I wanted to be an audio engineer. I didn't know much about it except what I learned along the way. You asked me how good I was; you'd just fired someone, and I was straight-up honest and told you where my skills were at. You told me you would allow me the time to learn if I came in and put in the work. I did that, but I couldn't work for you long because I had a lot going on at the time. You never once not picked up the phone or even not showed me love since that, and I appreciate you for that.

To my boy Lamar Ray Big Monte: You have been a big brother since day one; you never turned your back on me. You even taught me the art of coaching youth football and deserve your own book on it. Thank you for being in my corner.

To my boy Mike V: Thank you for being a part of this journey and all the wise words you bestowed upon me. You're like a big brother to me, and I appreciate you. From one single dad to another, I salute you.

To Alexis Perez and Bill Solomon of the Brooklyn Titans: I thank you for taking me in as family. Josiah loves playing for the Titans and I love coaching.

My boy Jamal who owns the deli on 135th and Springfield Blvd: You always made sure me and my kids had what we needed. You've been a hell of a friend and brother. Y'all always had my back since I've known y'all, and I want y'all to know I always had your back as well. This book is for us all.

To all my homies in Springfield Gardens looking out for me and the boys. My people in Southside Queens, my peoples in Corona. My homies in east New York, my peoples in Flatbush and Brownsville Brooklyn.

My peoples in Harlem: Mike, it's been nothing but love. You know I always got you and the girls; it's nothing but family love and vibes. You helped me level up.

My peoples in Columbia, South Carolina: Curtis, you know it's nothing but love from me; you always been a big brother. I know it's a lot more people I should be naming who were that was a big part of my journey.

Ashley, I have known you most of my life and you have never switched up. I love you forever, and thank you for always being solid.

I thank each and every one of you. This book is for all my peoples in the trenches, knee-deep in the blood and mud of it all.

Grind till you get everything you want. Find a lane and flip that money legally, start a business, get your LLC, and find your way out.

To all my real peoples behind them walls that stayed true: Hold your head. Your day is coming. Use that time wisely to make yourself better. Read and educate yourself. Don't come out the same person you went in. The world is already counting you out and expecting you to fail. Show the world you not going to let that situation define who you are; it's just a part of your story. Don't let them tell you there is no opportunity for you out here because you got a record. It's plenty if you can run a drug enterprise, you can run a business.

To all my fallen soldiers: I miss each and every one of y'all. I wish you was all here to enjoy this special moment with me. Rest in Power, T-mac, Boo Gotti, E, Peace, Goonie Ru, Bay G, Ricky, Fat Tommy, Ty, Tamekia. And everybody else we lost.

Last, but not least, most importantly, I wanna thank you, the reader. Though we don't know one another, I figured you'll learn what you need to about me in these pages, and since you picked up this book, I feel I know a few things about you as well. I hope my words can be an inspiration and you find healing you need and the strength to deal with whatever you're going through. This book is something I have been working on and wanting to do since I was fifteen years old. At the writing of this, that was thirteen years in the past. To see how far I've come is proof that it's never too late to do whatever you want to do. Embrace the struggle and embrace the journey. Don't be afraid to fail and try again. You never know what God has in store for you.

I hope you enjoy.

From my heart to your heart.

Chapter 1

The Diagnosis

When they asked us in first grade or kindergarten, I can't remember which it was, what we wanted to be when we got older, nobody ever said they wanted to be in the streets. Nobody ever said they wanted to be a drug dealer or a killer. Nobody ever said they wanted to be a felon. But somewhere along the journey, life puts you on a course that you'll have no control over. It's all part of the unpredictable way life goes, and unfortunately for some, that course, or that path, is a huge negative and could mean a life of torment, like mine was. Your environment and the circumstances you are in play a major role in the decisions on that journey, and for most children, or minors, there is no choice in your environment. Being born in South Central LA is a lot different from being born just a few miles across the way in Beverly Hills, but it's a whole different world of culture. Location is one thing, right? It isn't gonna change the fact that everyone has problems. For example, the better the upbringing a kid had, the more stability provided, and the more love that's given, the more likely that child will succeed in life. Or better yet, the more likely that child is going to grow into a life of happiness, which isn't always the same as succeeding. People can fail and still be happy, and those who succeed can find themselves in misery.

Some people just don't have a chance. The ones from the bottom who have everything stacked against and on top of them are those whose paths are multiple times harder than those with the silver spoon. It's a fact. I don't need to tell you the difference between a kid from the hood with less than two parents versus a kid in a crime-free suburban neighborhood who's already got a college fund started for them. Now, when the odds are stacked against you, like they were against me, it's almost a sense of luck to make it out of these fucked-up parts, but not like the sort of luck where you find a hundred dollars in a pair of jeans you haven't worn in a while. It's like being forced to play Russian Roulette and not dying.

There's a lot involved in a life and upbringing like mine that many don't understand, and I hate when people judge what they don't know or don't take the time to understand. If you ain't never walked a mile in a person's shoes or felt a person's struggle on your own level, how can you judge them or even form an opinion? The best lessons in life are those learned by experiences, by mistakes made, and by wounds healed. One thing I know well is pain, the physical, emotional, mental; whether I'm causing it or the one feeling it, I know pain. I'm from the jungle where you have to do whatever it takes to survive, and it has nothing to do with nature. Either you can be the hunter or you are the one getting hunted. It's predator or prey in these streets. And before you ask, there wasn't no options to sit inside and watch TV all day or play video games. The entire time you are going through these situations you don't realize it's fucking you up mentally. Because when you're fighting for your life, you are just in the moment and all you can think about is surviving.

Yeah, my story is fucked-up, but nowhere near the worst one you'll ever hear. Mine is just unique to my circumstances and the only one I'm fit to tell. I'm pretty sure everyone who deals with trauma over time finds their way to cope to make the pain bearable. My thing that I question is, do you ever escape the reality of that pain and trauma? Can you ever shake this disorder? I know everything starts with a thought. The fact is that I want to change. I want to elevate, and not just elevate myself, but elevate those around me. The only thing is, I HAVE TO CHANGE MY MINDSET.

Letting go of bad habits, negative thoughts, people who mean me no good, and escaping bad environments is one thing a person can do to alter their scenario. The thing is, do you really ever escape? I mean, you can outgrow an environment, but you're still a product of it, so it's in you; it's a part of your foundation. When you spend your life, your childhood, normalizing shit that ain't normal, it fucks you up, in a sense. Think about the first time you saw something traumatic: maybe someone got their ass beat; maybe someone got shot or stabbed. Hell, even if you are with someone and they are stealing something from the corner store—the first time you see it, it causes you to freeze and be like, "What the fuck? Where the fuck am I right now?" The second time you have an experience like that, it still makes you jittery, but after a while it just becomes regular life. The jitters fade out, the questions get answered; this is now normal. Well, that's why I'm writing this book, because I know so many people from the streets who have been through hell and want to move forward with their lives but still suffer from the aftereffects. I heard a quote once: "When you're in hell, don't stop; keep going. Why would you ever find yourself in hell and not keep pushing your way out?" The nightmares, the mentality of having to be a wolf in the woods, or a tiger in the jungle.

Sure, I know there are people who make it out with a hot song, a nice jump shot, or with some other skills. Yet, some of the ones who come from the streets still have a hard time elevating from the street mentality and escaping the traumas they encountered in their early stages of life. Unless they were blessed with a great support system. Look at the percentage of athletes and rappers that have been arrested or killed all because they kept their ties to the streets. They were blessed with the money and fame and still had a hard time leaving behind their past mentality. Now think about the average guy without money and fame that wants to elevate his mind and life beyond his environment and circumstances. It's twice as hard because you have to do it in the same environment under the same circumstance. How do you just adapt to everyday life? How do you just grow? How do you become a better 'you' in these harsh realities?

As I talk about my journey and where I'm headed, I hope it brings healing to any in need of it. This is a battle you have to win. It's a daily fight within yourself. You wanna change, but being this way got you this far. It's like, at first you try to figure shit out in the jungle, but the only way to survive is to be the beast. What are you gonna do? Become prey? Nah, that's not in my DNA, and if you are reading this book and you're anything like me, it isn't in yours either. So, you do whatever you have to do to survive, but in that comes a lot of traumas. You encounter a lot of shit, but you make it through, in a way.

It's always the question, 'Why me?' Survivor's remorse kicks in every now and then. Why did you choose to spare me, God? I catch myself thinking about the times it could have all been over. Closing my eyes, and feeling like I'm in that moment again, each shot felt like it was getting closer as we ran for cover. The bullets of my memories. When they finally stopped shooting and I got up, I saw somebody lying there choking on their own blood. I was just a little boy and I didn't know what to do. People ran up to him, panicking. My body froze like a complete ice statue in the Arctic. I just stared as people screamed for this person to stay up and fight. I wanted to run, but my legs couldn't move; I melted out of the fear and shock of it all.

That was the first time I ever saw a human die or get shot. I was nine years old, and, sad to say, it definitely wouldn't be my last time. Some people glorify the street life. Mostly it's the ones who were on the sidewalk and came out every now and then. For the ones who had nothing else, we wish there was another way. How many people have you seen shot? What memories leading up to your tenth birthday come back to you when you reminisce? Yeah, my journey made me, but the shit I had to experience left my mind with a disconnect.

As I'm getting older, I realize I am traumatized. The things that aren't supposed to be normal was normalized. Walking a thin line with death and jail was an everyday thing. The abuse delivered and received, and the things I had to do to survive it all. Something simple as robbing someone or even me being robbed, hurt someone or me being hurt. I can say, I'm blessed that I haven't been shot. But that doesn't mean nobody ever tried. I've been shot at, stabbed, cut, gotten my ass beat-up, and robbed. I've been betrayed by ones who I never thought would betray me, and I've been spared by some of my enemies. I have won fights, I lost fights, and I cheated when I had to. Imagine someone going through these things for years and years and expecting that person to be okay and adjust to the new world without fear or anxiety creeping in. Now, everyone's story ain't the same, and many of them are similar. But we are left with generations who suffer from PTSD, and the majority of it is undiagnosed. What happens when a soldier goes to war and experiences traumatic events? His partner killed in war, or him having to kill, or getting shot at. Watching bombs go off.

Usually when he or she comes back they label them with post-traumatic stress disorder, also known as PTSD.

What about the guy who has that traumatic experience from being in the streets? I know most will say one is more honorable and you don't have to be in the streets if you don't want to, but no one's been drafted into the military since the Vietnam war. What if I say they are almost the same and there are many similarities? Unlike the military, the streets aren't a choice for some; it's what you are forced into at a young age. When people get involved in the streets, some are recruited, and some choose to sign themselves up. Both feel like they are protecting their home turf. The military goes overseas to fight people who are against America's belief in democracy, or, they say, to keep the world peace. Is it over power, money, and resources? In the streets, you are against anybody who doesn't like the idea of what you stand for. There are many similarities, so to say one is good and one is bad, I personally can't agree with that. It's all based on your personal opinion and depends on who you ask and when you ask them. To the police, and the politicians, and the system, the people in the streets are nothing but thugs, and gangbangers, and drug dealers. To me, it's people who're lost and trying to find a way to survive. Many were born into these terrible fucked-up circumstances. If you go overseas and ask what some countries think of America, I'm willing to bet they'll have nothing nice to say.

See, me personally, I'm like most: a product of my environment. You stick a kid in foster care with no guidance, tell him to find his way and watch that lead to a path of destruction. By the age of sixteen, I was in juvenile detention for the third time in my life with my first time resulting in me doing two years in juvey at age eleven, going on twelve. Where were you when you were eleven? Where will your children be? I witnessed murders, rape, beatings, shootings, and lost people to senseless homicide, addictions, and suicides. I was never taught love, or that any of the things we were doing was wrong; all we wanted was a way out. As kids, you don't know there was more to life than what the streets gave us. The only love came from my bros who was going through the same things I was going through. We were doing everything we could to escape the harsh realities of our lives. That's what made the bonds grow.

None of the shit we encountered was normal. We didn't even realize we were supposed to seek help; we didn't know it was an option. Who cared for kids in the ghettos like us with no real family? No real support. When I was fifteen, I was diagnosed with post-traumatic stress disorder—and to think how wrong of an assessment that was! I'm older now; I know what stress is. Stress is a job, a mortgage payment, an argument you have with a loved one. No, I was not stressed. I was traumatized. My only disorder is I can't escape the trauma I suffered in the streets. Mentally. I am in counseling now. Does it work? For me it's all what you make it. Nobody has the answers to anyone's life. That person can only help you look deep within to find the answers. What I can say is it does help. It helps to have someone that doesn't know you listen as you try to sort the bullshit out in your head. For anybody that is looking to go, it's definitely worth a try. Search for one; every therapist is not the same. My advice would be go into it open-minded. For me, I'm willing to do anything to break the cycle and hope my kids never have to suffer from Post Traumatic Streets Disorder. I mean, I owe it to them. They saved me from myself, so it's only right I give them the best life possible. It's only right I elevate my mind and my life. Escape the environments that hold me back. I know if I don't, there is a strong possibility that they will follow in my footsteps. One thing I know: kids don't go off what you say; they go off what you do.

Chapter 2

The Long-Lost Journey

Seek you shall find
All wounds heal with time
Do you love me
Do you hate me
It's such a thin line

It took seventeen years, eleven months, and two weeks for me to learn the true meaning of unconditional love. It came at me in a single moment that I experienced a love I had never felt before. A feeling I never thought I would ever feel. I had come to a point where I actually wanted to keep on living. This event that I speak of was the birth of my son, Josiah, and the very moment that added purpose to this journey called life. I finally had reason to live and I came to a point where I wanted to be alive. Before that point, I did not care much about anything at all; the only thing that mattered to me then was getting money. Money was freedom; money made people love you. Growing up, I idolized the guys in the streets. To me, they had freedom, they had the money, and it just seemed like they had it all figured out.

Before I could even understand what was going on, I knew I wanted to be a part of that lifestyle. I was introduced to the street life at an early age, and there was no other opportunity or guidance keeping me from it. I remember when I was seven and a half; I was in a foster home, one of a few I would live in throughout my childhood. My foster mother at the time was a damaged woman. Any time she went out, she would only buy her daughter toys and snacks from the store. I wanted toys; I wanted snacks. But no— like thousands of other young foster children in this country, I was just a paycheck for this woman. The first time I went in the store with her, I was excited; I figured this would be my chance to get something. She bought her daughter some candy. I asked for a piece of candy for myself and she looked me dead in my eyes and said, "You not my child; the State only pays me just enough to feed your ass and make sure your orphan ass got somewhere to sleep." This was the environment I was given. No love, no compassion, no guidance—only hostility and obligation.

One Sunday after church, we went to the store, and as usual, I was not getting anything. It was raining on this particular Sunday and my foster mom did not feed us before church. She said we was taking too long to get dressed and we left the house without a meal. By the time we got in the store, I was really hungry; I hadn't eaten since dinner the evening before. We had to be in bed by 7:30 p.m. on Saturdays. So, you can imagine what time we ate, and it was already past lunch. It was afternoon time. I asked her could I get something. She ignored me. So, I asked again, "Please can I get something?" Still no answer. I took her ignoring me as a yes. I walked up to the chips and grabbed them and took them to her. That woman slapped me so hard I forgot how to breathe for a few seconds, and she told me to get out the store. You best believe her daughter got that exact bag of chips bought for her. On the way home, my foster mom told her daughter, "You better not give him none or it is going in the trash." And I don't blame the daughter. I know she wanted to give me some and share; she wasn't a bad person. But I wanted her to eat as well. All my foster mom kept saying was, "That is why nobody want your dirty black ass. That's the reason you ain't no damn good. You lucky I need this money I am getting for you." She made sure to let me know every day that I did not belong. This was not the first, or last, time I went through this.

During the summer when school wasn't in, she would send me outside in the afternoons. It was a hatred she had for my existence I felt. At first, before I made friends I would just hang out at the park for a while trying to catch some shade, and sometimes I'd walk to the corner. That was where these guys would always be hanging out. Older guys, I thought they were pretty cool at the time, and wondered if their moms kicked them out the house for the same reasons I had been. I was hungry one day; I walked by the guys and went in the store to steal a Swiss Roll and Zebra Cake. I would do this often and usually get away with it. When I got outside, one of the guys called me over and asked me why I stole that out the store. I replied, "I'm hungry, and I can't go home." He was like, "Word, I respect that." He then pulled out a bunch of money and gave me ten dollars. He told me, "Wait right here." He went in the store and brought me a sandwich and a juice. I was thankful for the sandwich and to be eating. All I could think about while I chomped through my sandwich was how much money I seen and how he helped me with that money. That was a power I hadn't yet fully understood. I knew then with just that glimpse, money makes a difference. I knew, at a young age, I had to have money when I got older. And I knew I wanted the money.

My time at that particular foster home and outside would be spent playing with other kids and watching the guys on the corner, mimicking their language and their movements. There was one day at the park my stomach was hurting bad. I really had to go to the bathroom. I rushed home, and I knocked on the door.

After knocking for what felt like an hour but probably was really like five minutes, she finally came to the door and yelled, "What you want, boy?" I replied, "I really got to go to the bathroom." She yelled back, "You a boy; whip your thing out and pee." I yelled back, "I don't have to pee." She yelled, "Boy, if you don't get from in front my door—" I said, "Please, my stomach hurts. I'm about to use the bathroom on myself." "Get ya ass from in front my damn door and don't let me say it again." I couldn't hold it no more and used the bathroom on myself. "I doo-doo on myself!" I yelled out, crying from the discomfort and embarrassment of it all. "Come back in a couple hours and get your nasty stink ass in the shower." Being starved, being beat, and feeling no love was something I came accustomed to. But not letting a little boy use the bathroom and making him walk the day in his own shit is torture. And I can't help but think that's what she wanted. I took my shirt off and wrapped it around my waist and left. I went back down the stairs and tried to stay as far as I could away from the other kids, in the hopes they wouldn't discover what I did. It was impossible and I was not successful. See, adults and normal folk, they'd be mortified to find out what I had gone through. I get it; sometimes people piss themselves or shit themselves in movies and TV and it's a big laugh. In a situation like this, no one should laugh, and if they did, my explanation of the scenario would cut off the humor right away. But not with kids in the hood I was in. You do something crazy, you are going to get embarrassed. That's exactly what happened. One of the older kids seen the way I was walking. He ran up to me and said, "Why are you walking like that?" I tried to say my leg hurt, but it was like he knew. He called his other friends over and they all started picking on me. I got mad and punched one of the kids after he pushed me. They all started hitting me, and when I hit the ground, they started kicking me while I was down. When they stopped hitting me, I just felt angry, and for the first time, I wished I were dead. I hated my life. I hated where I lived, I had really no friends, and I got jumped because I couldn't go to the bathroom and had to use it on myself.

I knew that if I had the money like the guy on the corner, stuff like that wouldn't happen to me anymore. I hated living in her house; I didn't even have a bed most nights. Some nights, I didn't get to eat, and she had this rod she would use to beat me.

The Rod. Was a small metal one. Boy, did that rod hurt. Every hit was like getting cut on your skin. When it hit me, my skin would have burned even with clothes on. Imagine how it felt with no pants on and the scars and welts it left me with. She had an older son who was about twenty-one at the time, and two daughters. One was fifteen and the other was nine. It was three rooms in the house. Her room, the boy's room, and the girls' room. The room had one bed. See, when I first got over there it was me and her two daughters and sometimes her boyfriend or other guys she would try to hide, but I'd seen them anyway. On some nights when I first got there, things were okay. I got to sleep in the bed and had the room to myself as long as she wasn't mad. My foster mom would only be mad when she and the boyfriend argued or fought, which was all the time. She didn't have too many happy moments. Mostly putting on a front and pretending for people. I remember one day; it was her younger daughter's ninth birthday. My foster mother threw a party.

I was always in awe of other kids' birthday parties growing up because I'd never had a birthday party myself, not once. Growing up, I would have to close my eyes and imagine the type of party I wanted to have. What cartoon characters I wanted, what my cake would look like, and what color balloons I would like to have. At her daughter's party, it seemed normal. The adults were laughing and having a good time, the kids were playing, everyone seemed happy. Me and one of the boys at the party started fighting over one of the toys. At the time, I didn't know it was my foster mother's nephew. She and her sister ran over after I pushed the boy down and he started crying. First, the boy's mother snatched me up and said, "Keep ya hands off my fucking child." Then POW she smacked me in my face and kept yelling, then hit me again and threw me on the ground like I was dirty laundry. She embraced her child, consoled him, and sent him to go back and play. My foster mother grabbed me and said to me, "See? I can't bring your ass nowhere." And she hit me too, and told me to sit down by myself for the remainder of the day. Even though this was all I knew, I could tell, at that age, that this wasn't the way a kid should be treated. After all, I had witnessed my foster mom's sister treat her son, the one I pushed, with kindness while he cried. After that whole deal, my foster mom told me, "Don't worry about no cake or ice cream." Which might have been the worst part of the whole situation.

For the remainder of the party, I had to sit down in the corner, not allowed to speak or move, and watch the kids play games. I was given a hot dog and a juice, which was the least they could do, but I bet if there weren't other people there, my foster mom would have made me go hungry. When it was time to sing "Happy Birthday," I had to watch from the table. She really did not give me any cake or ice cream, and I was furious because I really wanted some. I barely got to eat at the house, hearing cake and ice cream… getting to experience that wouldn't have made up for all the birthday parties I never got, but at least I still would have got some. I spent my time watching the adults and I could tell my foster mother was mad about something. When we got home after the party, and after me watching the kids have fun, I heard her ask her boyfriend, "So you just going to disrespect me in my face?" as she lit her cigarette. He replied, "Don't start your shit; I'm about to go." She snapped back at him, "That's all you do, anyway, is leave. You're never here; maybe I should get another man over here." I had no idea, but I was about to learn something in the next few moments, and to this day, I cannot tell you what that thing I learned was. Trauma will do that to you. After she snapped back at him, all I heard was a loud boom and she screamed; she yelled, "What are you hitting me for? I'm sorry!" she yelled out. He replied, "You want another man?" Barely being able to respond like she was getting choked, she said "No!" He yelled out, "I will kill you! Don't ever say no shit like that." We heard another hit and another hit and then he walked to the bathroom, not even looking in our direction. Seeing her get beat, a part of me felt bad for her. Then the other part of me felt like, 'good for her,' because of how she used to do me. I did used to hate seeing people hurt. The first time it happened I was a little scared because I thought someone was going to die. I didn't know how to react; as child, I didn't know if that was normal or not. Up until that point, I never had a man tell me boys hitting girls is bad. I had to learn that along the way, like many of the lessons I learned early in life.

Later on that night, I was in the room with the girls, which I was not allowed to be in. The youngest was crying and her big sister was hugging her, trying to calm her down after everything that went on. The older sister was used to her mama going through things like this, and later on when they got into it, it would often remind her. I heard the door close, which meant the boyfriend had left. So, I walked out the room and found my foster mother on the kitchen floor, crying. Her lip was busted, and she was shaken-up. I felt something for her then, and the child in me didn't fully understand the situation. I asked her if she was okay. She looked me dead in my eyes and said, "Get your ass out of here and mind your business." I imagine she felt the weakness she made me feel all those times, and if she hadn't been so beat-up, I bet she would have hit me and busted my lip. I was right. I don't know what came over her, but she had this look in her eyes and said, "I thought I told your ass to never go in the girls' room." Before I could tell her that her oldest daughter told me to come in there, she hopped up and smacked me in my face twice. She went and grabbed the rod and started to whip me with it. It was obvious that she wasn't mad at me; that frustration of hers had to go somewhere. After she got done, she sent me in the room for the rest of the night. She said, "You are lucky I don't make your ass sleep outside."

This was a night I will remember until the day I die. All I could think about in the room while I was crying was, 'Why was she mad at me?' I grabbed a pencil and paper and wrote down on a piece of paper, *I hate my life, I hate it here, I wish I was dead. Nobody loves me.* That may have been when I became a writer; pretty fucked-up, but I turned it around for my growth, and here I am writing this book. Later that night, I felt somebody shaking me to wake up. It was her oldest daughter. She said, "Ssshhh…" She said, "I'm sorry I got you beat. I hate her too." She asked if I was ok. I shook my head yes, even though my back and legs were still hurting from the beating her mom gave me with the rod. Then out of nowhere she kissed me on my mouth. I'd only seen that done on TV or by adults. I just stared at her, and she got in the bed with me. She said to me, "Don't be scared." She kissed me again but this time she put her tongue in my mouth. She lifted her shirt and bra and told me to kiss on her breast. I did. She took my hand and placed it on her private area. She was moving my hand around. I didn't know what was going on, but I could tell she liked it. This went on for a little while. Eventually, she moved my hand, pulled down her shirt and said, "You better not tell nobody." And she walked out the room. It wouldn't be the last time she snuck inside my room. This happened quite a few times. I know now that it was sexual abuse I was experiencing. I can't really know why she did what she did. I wondered at times if she had ever been abused herself, or what led her to do to me what she did. If you haven't realized yet, I was not in a safe place.

I know some of y'all are reading this and asking yourselves, "What about her son?" and, "How did Justin end up sleeping on the floor?" Her older son was in prison when I first got there and was released a few months after. I remember one time when her and her boyfriend was fighting, she told him, "Wait until my son gets home." I also wondered where he was at so he could help her. The fighting between my foster mom and the boyfriend became normal to me and I just minded my business because I did not want to feel that rod and I didn't want to miss any meals. I was learning. She would still find reasons to beat me with it even when I was good. So, I did the best I could do to stay out her way. I would watch TV. My favorite movie I would watch over and over was *Free Willy*. I always wish I was like Jesse. We had similar stories growing up in foster care, except I was never waiting on my mother to come get me. I wished I could have people in my life like he did. I also used to look forward to going outside. I hated being in the house with her and the cigarette smoke.

The first time her son walked through the door, my foster mom screamed and gave him the biggest hug I'd ever seen. I didn't even know she was capable of such affection. The son walked up to his sisters, and he gave the older sister a hug and asked if she had a boyfriend. She laughed and told him to "mind your business." He told her, "Don't get none of these boys hurt." She rolled her eyes. He picked his little sister up and said, "I missed you so much." This feeling of family and happiness was something I wasn't used to. I was sitting on the couch, and he looked over at me and said "Ma, is that the boy you tried to replace me with?" She replied, "I will never replace you; I just needed extra money from the State. It was expensive sending your ass money, and these damn bills are high." He laughed and walked up to me and said, "What up, little nigga?" I said, "What's up?" He walked to the room and put his bag down. He started yelling out from the room, "Mama, where I'm going sleep?" She shouted back to him, "Boy, don't you aggravate me. That's your room; ain't shit changed." My foster mother had to go to the supermarket, so she headed out to the store. I walked in the room to go get a toy my caseworker had got me. He grabbed me and yoked me up and told me to stay out his way and to mind my business. He told me don't touch nothing of his and he took my stuff out the dresser and threw it in the closet. "Man, whatever you do, don't touch my shit." He made sure I understood he would fuck me up bad if I touched his stuff. I said to him, "You just touched *my* stuff." Then he punched me in the chest really hard. I dropped to my knees instantly, tears dropping from my eyes. It felt like I stopped breathing momentarily. He looked at me and said, "You too soft; you can't sleep in this room if you going to be so fucking soft. Quit crying," he yelled, "before I punch you again." I stopped, the best I could.

The first time he ever took me outside was the moment I began to idolize him. His mother made him take me. She had something to do with the girls that day at the church and was not about to leave me in the house by myself. When we got outside, and we got to the corner, I saw him walk up to the guys that I would watch on the corner. They did this handshake. Not too much later, I found out that was a gang handshake for the Bloods. I heard one of the guys ask, "You babysitting now, son?" He replied, "Hell no, Moms told me to take him with me!" He called me over and told me take my ass to the park and stay there until he come gets me. I didn't listen and ended up back at the store after a while. He got on me for that, but he ended up having to go somewhere and took me with him.

That day while we were together, he told me, "Whatever you see is not to be talked about, or I'll knock all your teeth out your mouth." I saw him pick something up, take it somewhere, and get some money. He did that a few times. I was learning, even though I didn't realize it. He let me use his CD player; he had the DMX CD in there. I will never forget the song that was playing. It's still my favorite DMX song. Well, one of my favorite songs of all times: "Slipping." I may not have known all the words or understood them at the time. I did understand, "I'm slipping I'm Falling I can't get up." I felt the pain. I loved music. My favorite thing to do was try and remember the lyrics and be able to recite them without the music on. I would rap the songs I could remember when I was scared or after some type of beating or punishment. This skill would help me all throughout my life, even in adulthood. While being incarcerated, especially in solitary confinement. I would go through as much of an album as my brain would let me. It was like a game to me, and it passed time.

Things took a turn for the worse one night when my foster mother and her boyfriend was arguing and fighting. He stopped coming around as much after her son came home from prison. They probably only had seen each other twice. When the son came home, the boyfriend would leave. Her son did not like him at all, and for good reasons. He used to tell his mother he is going to hurt him one day. She would reply, "No, you not, you not going back to jail." I could hear the worry in her voice. She was at risk of losing one of the men in her life.

On this particular night, her son came in earlier than usual. I was in the living room playing with my toys. He walked through the door and went into his room. Then he came back into the kitchen. Her son didn't have to ask for anything in the kitchen. Only me and her two daughters did. Her many house rules did not apply to him. He was in the kitchen fixing himself a sandwich when the door was opened. We heard my foster mom and the boyfriend arguing. She walked toward the kitchen and stopped dead in her tracks when she realized her son was home. I don't think the boyfriend knew either, otherwise he wouldn't have been raising his voice like he was. He looked at his mama and knew instantly something was wrong. "Ma, you alright?" he asked, and she didn't reply. He didn't even finish asking the question when he ran up to her boyfriend. He started with, "What you do?" … and before he finished his sentence, he punched the boyfriend in the face. Her boyfriend grabbed him, and they started wrestling. Then next thing I know, I heard her yell to her boyfriend, "Oh my god, you are bleeding!" He stopped, he looked … it was blood coming through his shirt. Her son stabbed him a couple times; you can tell he was in prison working his knife because it happened so fast. No one even saw when he grabbed the knife. Especially the boyfriend. I don't know if him seeing the knife would have changed the results of what happened. He never stood a chance. It took a couple of stabs and my foster mother yelling out for him to realize he was stabbed. When he realized he had been stabbed, he grabbed his side and let out a scream, "Aw shit, you stabbed me, lil nigga." I remember her son; his shirt was ripped, he yelled at the boyfriend, "You better leave before I kill your ass." The way he started bleeding I didn't think he had far to go until he was dead.

My foster mother picked up the phone and called 9-1-1. I heard her tell them, "A man is outside laying down. I think these boys attacked him and stabbed him." She lied. The boyfriend stumbled out the door. Me and her older daughter cleaned up the blood. That was the first time I had someone else's blood on my hands. While no one was looking, the daughter kissed me and laughed. After that whole situation, the son stayed away from the house for a couple of days, and I got to sleep in the bed for a bit. My foster mother became much meaner after that, and it wasn't entirely directed at me. Her older daughter, the one who would sneak into my room, ended up running away after they got in a fight one day. I don't know exactly where she went but my guess would be probably to her boyfriend's house or one of her friends' houses. The fight all started when my foster sister walked through the door. After her curfew. My foster mother was drinking— probably already drunk. She asked her, "Where the fuck you been?" Her daughter replied, "I'm home now." I knew my foster mother was not going to let that comment go. "Who the fuck you talking to?" Before her daughter could respond, she got up, snatched her by the hair. She slammed her against the wall and put her hand around her neck. She told her, "If you ever talk to me again like that it will be the last thing you ever fucking say, you little bitch." My foster sister ran in her room and stayed in there and when her mama fell asleep, she left. This time for good. I hated to see her go; she was cool and took care of me and her little sister when her mother was occupied with a man or gone or too drunk. Before the fight, I just had got a beating for asking what's for dinner and telling her I was hungry. That night, after the fight, she sent me to lie on my spot on the floor and fed her daughter (the youngest child). She would make me sleep on the floor because she said since I wanted to act like an animal, she was gonna treat me like one. There would be nights with no dinner, due to something I did or didn't do during the day. Sometimes there'd be no reason at all. I felt my foster mom enjoyed the pain she caused me. What other explanation can there be? Eventually, I had started sneaking cold cuts out the fridge. I had it all planned out, knew where to step, and would open the door so slowly, not a sound was made. I was like a ninja; I had to be. I wouldn't even breathe when I had to sneak food; it was worth too much. One night, I got caught and she hit me so hard in my mouth it began to bleed. She'd knocked my tooth out my mouth. She made me tell my case worker it happened when I was riding a bike. The caseworker was stupid; I didn't even have a bike. He never even checked her story. When not feeding me wasn't enough punishment, she grabbed the rod and went to work on my legs or found creative ways to punish me. I kept stealing food from the fridge after that. I just got better at it.

One day, I was with my case worker, and I said, "If I don't go to my mommy and daddy, I will kill myself." I never knew my parents; the closest thing I had to a family was a foster home I been in and out of since I was two and a half. The Reeves family. They would put me in the Reeves family after they took me from an aunt from one of my birth parents' sides. It was told to me she abused me as a baby until the point I was hospitalized. They would take me out the Reeveses' house, then put me back and take me back out. Over and over. I will explain more in the next chapter. Little did I know that experience changed my whole childhood. I was never a happy child growing up; I always felt like I didn't belong. Even before these experiences in this foster home. I felt empty inside. That foster home I was in had a lot to do with my journey. It was the beginning of me taking a walk on the long-lost journey.

Chapter 3

The Trauma

It got really bad at that foster home after my foster mother's son stabbed her boyfriend. It's like she became angry, bitter, and we were all her enemies after that. She took it out on everyone. I guess it didn't matter how bad her boyfriend treated her; she would rather have him and all the bad that came with him than be alone. Thinking of it now as a grown man knowing what I know, there's no way she loved him. I know he definitely didn't love her. He loved the power he had over her, the way she needed him, and she loved the idea of just having someone and not feeling alone. She loved the fact there was a man there paying her bills. Now all of that was gone. My foster mother and her older daughter began fighting a lot. Her older daughter would be gone for weeks after they fought. At first, they would fight after a while. She knew it was nothing she could do to control her teenage daughter. She even stopped going to church.

She quit cooking. She probably cooked twice a week if we were lucky. After the stabbing, her son stopped coming over there like that. He came over twice, to be exact. He came to grab the things he needed, like his clothes or to grab some food. I'm not sure if it's because he was trying to lay low and avoid the police after her boyfriend told them what happened, or if he was just trying to avoid his mother. When he used to be around, he would take me with him to his girlfriend's house. He taught me how to defend myself by making me slap box and fight other kids. I even got to be with him while he made his money. I saw how he hustled; he even showed how a man is supposed to treat a woman. Now that I think about it, a man is not supposed to treat a woman the way he did her. He used to smack her and make her have sex in front of his friends and in front of me. I didn't know that was wrong at the time; my own experience with sex was one I never asked for. It was what it was to me, and I normalized it. They were all laughing and seemed to be enjoying the way he treated her. It was like people feared him; not too many people ever told him 'no.' He was fearless in everything he did until he went back to jail. I don't know if it was for the stabbing or different charges.

I just heard when my foster mother at that time said, "You got your ass back in there; find a way. You on your own." She slammed the phone on the hook so hard you would have thought she was trying to hit him with it through the phone. Over the months, I looked up to him like a big bro. Even if he was a bad example, at least he was the only one taking the time to be an example at that time. I had to get out of there once her son went back to jail. I would have rather died than be at that house.

In the previous chapter, I stated how I got out that foster home by telling my caseworker, "If you don't take me out of that home and give me back to mommy and daddy, I will kill myself." Would I have did it? Probably not. I just felt like death was a better option. Even as a child with my whole life ahead of me. That did not matter; the pain I was carrying around felt like too much to bear. So, I told them how I felt and where I would rather be. No, the Reeves wasn't my real parents, but they treated me better than any other foster home I been to and was the only ones who at least tried to make me a part of their family. With the Reeves family, I had brothers, aunties, uncles, and cousins. Once I said that I would kill myself, they took me to a hospital to evaluate me. I had to talk to different people, and they asked me a lot of questions. To see what was going on and why I felt the way I felt. I never went into details of what was going on. I just kept saying I hate it there I want my mommy and daddy.

When I was saying I want my mommy and daddy at that time, I wasn't referring to the Reeves family. I was talking about my real mother and father, the ones who made me. It was something I could never have. I was told when I was younger one day after asking for them that my parents were dead. There were many times in my life I wanted my birth parents. Well, mostly my birth mother, and I couldn't have her. That thought always left me with an empty feeling and many questions. Like, why did my mother leave me? Why wasn't I loved? I mostly felt unwanted and incomplete. My caseworker at child services notified the Reeves family what was going on with me. They went and got a lawyer so they could get me back into their home. Something they would remind me of often and throw in my face many times growing up. After going to court, the judge eventually put me back with the Reeves family at their house in Queens, but the damage was done. I was exposed to so much pain and the only ones who would show me love in that hell of a situation was the guys on the corner, and, at times, her son when he was there.

Out of all the foster homes I've been in, only one was decent. It was the Reeves family home. Besides the one I told you about earlier in the book. The other ones I have been in was a stay for a few weeks, even sometimes days, then I would be off to the next home. The Reeves family, they would eventually adopt me at ten and a half, almost eleven, and even change my name. By the way, I hate that they changed my name; it was like they took my identity away. I went from David Earl Williams to Justin David Reeves. The Reeves had one son together, James Jr., and my adopted mother had a son from a previous relationship, Jamalh. Me and James never really got along; even till this day as grown men, we don't really speak. I really don't even look at him as a brother because he never treated me like one. Me and Jamalh was always tight; he will always be my brother. I would give him my last or even the shirt off my back, even though he can't fit it.

Jamalh and Big James did not get along. Jamalh was kicked out of the house. I had to be about six years old when he and my foster father got into a fight in the kitchen. I was knocked out of the chair during that fight, like when one of those cartoon tornado battles sucks up all the innocent bystanders. I didn't even understand too much why they were fighting at that time, either. I would guess because Jamalh never liked her husband, and Big James, my adopted father, didn't like him because he was heavily involved in the streets. I felt like he thought he was better than him. I don't know the real reason. My adopted father took that grudge to the grave with him when he passed. I remember, the night they fought, I sat at the table to eat and all I heard was my foster father say, "You not gonna disrespect me in my own fucking house." And next thing I know, they're fighting and I'm on the floor. The chair I'm talking about is not a regular dining room chair. It's like a tall bar stool a few feet up off the ground and I was little for my age. It was a long, hard fall. After Jamalh left again, I was being left home with James, who was only like four years older than me. His favorite thing to do was get me in trouble, get me beatings, and laugh at me while it was happening. I wasn't the only foster child they would bring into their house. They had a revolving door for foster kids at this place. I would be the only one that they eventually adopted. Of all the people who came in through those doors, the

Spanish one was probably the coolest besides the little baby. But the Spanish one didn't last long, and he got put out for beating up their son. The son deserved it.

One day, I got in a fight with one of the foster kids who was older that came in the home. That's what let me know I could defend myself and wasn't scared to do so. It boosted my confidence so much. The way it happened was, my foster parents gave me and James a Nintendo 64. The new foster kid had a PlayStation. I wanted to play so bad! He would always say no. On this particular day, he let me play. I did not even think about it, I had my hands on the controller so fast. Next thing I knew, he pulled his pants down and said to me, "If you wanna keep playing, you need to touch it and give it a kiss." I told him, "No, boys don't do that." He walked up to me and said, "What did I say?" He tried to grab me to force me to do it and I pushed him. He must not have liked that, because he punched me in my stomach. I grabbed my stomach and bent over. When he walked up to me, I punched him back; he didn't like that and he let me have it. He started punching and punching. For every five hits he was getting, I would get like one, but I did not back down. I wouldn't. I knew what he was trying to get me to do wasn't right. I was not afraid to stand up for myself. I lost; well, actually speaking, I got my ass kicked, but I was able to stand up for myself.

That situation only made it worse. I was damaged early. I was exposed to a lot of foul shit early. I saw things I was never supposed to see as a kid growing up. Violence, Domestic Violence, Death,

Rape, and Drugs. When you are a kid, though, you don't know what is what. You just go as you're told and adapt to your environment. Most of the time I didn't ask to see none of that shit; I was exposed to it. By the time I hit fourth grade, I had to be about nine years old at the time, it was like a switch went off in my head. I didn't give a fuck no more.

I stopped caring and started acting up in school. I will never forget the day. A boy was teasing me about being ashy and dirty. I just got up out of my seat and punched him in the face and walked out of class. I don't know what had me so angry or made that switch flip. It could have been the crazy summer I had or because of the courtroom sessions I had to go to. If I had to guess, I would say the night before that day was part of the cause for my anger. I can never forget the night before. I broke a bowl on accident in my adopted parents' house and Big James got really mad. He made sure I understood that any given moment they could 'give me back to the State and that I belong to the State.' I was not adopted yet at this time. He reminded me my mama was dead, and my daddy was dead, and nobody else would want me. Then he whipped my ass.

When I got back to the Reeveses' home sometime in the fourth grade, the damage was far past done. In school, I used to walk around the class, never sitting still, doing whatever I wanted. The teachers eventually just ignored me. I walked out of class when I wanted to and walked around the school when I wanted to. My foster parents had me in an afterschool program, but I ended up getting kicked out after a while. I did not listen. I always ended up doing what I wanted to do. If you put me to stand in time-out in the corner, I was the kid who would sit down when I wanted and got up when I wanted. One day, I was walking around the school, being a badass little fourth-grade kid, and I was going up the back hallway and I heard a cry, "No, stop!" Of course, I went to investigate. I kept going up the stairs and I turned the corner to go up the next flight of stairs. That's when I saw a girl sitting on the steps with two boys surrounding her. One boy in front of her and the other on the side of her. The one in front of her had his hand in her shirt. The other one had his hands in her pants between her legs. The one with his hand down her shirt grabbed her by the neck. I froze and just stared at them. By this time in my life, I knew exactly what was going on and I could tell she was uncomfortable. I don't know the age or even if they went to the school. She looked at me and said, "Just go away." But I kept looking. One of the boys got sick of me watching and told me to get out of there and go back to class. I didn't move and I just stared. I was frozen; I don't know why. One of the guys came over to me and punched me in the stomach and chest told me to 'mind my fucking business' and pushed me down the stairs. I never knew what happened after that; I got up and got out of there. At different points in my life, especially in my childhood, there were moments I would be helpless, and I wanted to do so much to stand up and fight for myself. After that instance, I would start sticking up for myself. I would win some fights, lose some fights, and cheated when I had to. I just wasn't going to be weak and let people feel like they can punk me. I also learned fast to mind my business. I would fight as much as I could. Fight whoever, whenever; it didn't matter. I fought a lot of older boys coming up. They were the easiest to pick fights with. I can honestly admit that I started off losing more than I won. I was never scared to fight, though; I never wanted to back down. The more I hung out outside, the more trouble I got into in school. I was learning all the bad habits and it was growing into my personality. I would disturb class so often and so bad, they ended up putting me in Special Ed. I had to go to another school. I did the same thing there. I just didn't care about anything then. I didn't care if I came or went. If I was alive or not.

Fast-forward to 2021, real fast.

"You have a prepaid call from a federal inmate; you will not be charged for this call. To decline, hang up. To accept, press 5." Me, I'm going to always press 5 even if I have to pay for it. This time calling is my adopted mother's older son from a previous relationship. My brother Jamalh in a federal prison doing a thirty-two-year sentence for a bank robbery he committed when he was twenty-four years old. He has been locked up for twenty years and still got another eight if they don't pass any new laws. He's been in there since I was eight years old. Not one time did I ever look at his situation and say, "Damn, I don't wanna end up like that." Not one time did it ever scare me into doing right. I just thought whatever dumb shit he did I won't make the same mistakes. 'I'll be smarter than him.' This phone call, he was in good spirits. It sounded like he had hope he was getting out, like it was for sure this time. He told me they were about to change the gun laws and he would get his time cut down. Every time before he hangs up, he always lets me know it wasn't worth it. The little time he had balling was not worth the time he lost. He just wanted to be rich and put his family in a decent position; that was his reasoning. All he wanted was a way out of the fucked-up predicament he was in. He wanted off the block, wanted out the hood.

Isn't that what we all wanted? Hanging up the phone with him now always makes me reflect on my journey and makes me think that if I was born into a rich family, hell, even a stable one with great support, I wouldn't have embarked on the journey I went on. I probably would have turned out much better. My path probably wouldn't have been destructive, or as destructive.

I was born traumatized. My birth mother brought me into the most fucked-up situation a baby can be brought into. My mama had a very strong drug addiction. It was so bad, she smoked crack throughout her entire pregnancy with me. When I was born, I had crack in my system and almost died. She could have smoked crack the day I was born; I'll never know. So, technically, I was born high on drugs. With crack in my system, I was given to the State. Did you know that babies nowadays who are born to heroin- or opiate-addicted mothers need to be weaned off the drug? The nurses and doctors have to put morphine into their mouths, as infants, to wean them off the heroin in their blood. I have been fighting, since birth, a lot of pain, a lot of traumas, but still I remain.

Chapter 4

Off the Sidewalk

A lot of people think, or say, that getting involved in the streets is a choice. To me, that statement is only partially right. Technically speaking, everything you do in life is a choice. So, in them terms they are correct. I say partially to that because for some, the streets are a vacuum. Especially when you are young. It sucks you right in. It's something that just happens; you see an escape. A chance to make your life so much better than what it is. Especially when your life is as messed-up as mine was turning out to be.

You usually don't start out with robbing someone, or shooting at someone, or wanting to be some gangsta. Like I said in Chapter 1: Nobody, when they were in kindergarten, or first grade, said they wanted to be or do anything related with the streets. You usually start off as just a regular badass kid or hanging with the badass kids. I know for me, and many like me, that's what it was. Every bad choice just leads to a worser one. One day you can be playing tag; the next it might be ringing doorbells and running, or throwing rocks at windows and cars. One day you are stealing bikes just because you don't have one and your parent or parents can't afford one. There are days you are outside all day hungry. Now the hunger got you thinking of ways just to get something to eat and drink. You and your friends come up with a plan to steal from the store or from someone. All the endless ideas just to come up with money. All the badass dares you do just to prove you can fit in; that you not no punk. I say that to say it's all buildups along the journey.

You can go to any prison in America and find that for 99 percent of the ones convicted of murder, that was not their first crime, even if that's the first one they were caught for. Nobody wants to do bad or struggle in life. The things you see and experience in your environment, the things you go through at school growing up, all play a roll. It all influences your decisions. Most the kids coming from backgrounds like mine, where else is there for them to turn? When life at home is messed-up and you don't have much of anything, not even support. Where do you go to? When you're grown, yeah, you begin to understand the consequences behind every action, and you have alternative routes. You can go to work when you are an adult, find some type of way. You can also choose to give up on life, you can become homeless and beg for money if you want; you don't have to be a criminal. When you're a child, especially one without a father figure, without the proper guidance, you see the hustlers outside who get money and they look like the rappers on TV. You begin to idolize them. You know the money can change whatever it is that you're dealing with. Well, at least I did. I idolized the drug dealers, and the gangstas. Call it weird, but I knew I wanted to always be someone who got money. I loved the rappers who were actually from that life and told the story. Growing up in my early years, I never idolized rappers or people on TV. The problem for me was the dudes on TV lived in mansions outside of the hood. In a way, the rappers were acting the part to sell records to the people in the hood; they no longer were living the life, and some of them never lived the life at all and was just around.

So, every time I was outside, I got to be around the streets, I was around it. I was there soaking up the knowledge, absorbing the lifestyle. When I was told to fight, I didn't think twice. I was swinging even if they were bigger than me. I didn't care; like I said in the previous chapter, I won some fights, I lost some fights, and I cheated when I had to. I just wasn't scared to fight. The older guys grew to love me. I was a little soldier in training. Like I said early in the chapter. I was just starting off as just being a badass kid. It was three other kids I hung with every day. If one fought, we all fought. At nine years old is when I really started to get my feet wet. It was the summer before my tenth birthday. Before the summer, all I did was steal snacks from stores and we would fight other kids, and that was pretty harmless, considering what came next. That summer, we started hanging out with this Spanish kid who was older than us. He had to be thirteen-turning-fourteen at the time. He took me on my first home invasion. We waited for this one family to leave the house one day. There was a kid that lived there who used to always talk to us from out the window and show us his toys. His mother would never let him play with us; she probably thought we were a bad influence. One day, the three of us, we climbed through the window. The Spanish kid told us to take what we wanted. The Spanish kid went through the house. Two of us just grabbed some toys and ran out the house. We met back up at the park later and the Spanish kid showed us what he got. He took some money. We were all excited; we didn't even think to take more than the toys. But since we had some cash, we went to the store and got some snacks. That summer was a wild summer. It would also be the first time I smoked weed. It would be the first time I seen someone get killed. All these things I wasn't supposed to be exposed to, I was exposed to before I was even a teenager. I say it was a wild summer, but it was all part of the trauma that was my childhood.

When I was almost eleven, my foster family decided to leave New York City and relocate Down South. They thought the South was a better place to raise a family and it would keep us out of trouble. As they would soon learn, trouble should have been my nickname because it seemed to follow me wherever I went to. Moving Down South was like stepping into another planet. Now we lived in an apartment with a park, a pool, and a basketball court. I hated every bit of it. I missed my friends. I missed New York. It wouldn't be long before I found myself in trouble Down South and found a group of kids older than me who didn't care about anything, just like I ain't care. Fighting kids in my apartment complex and going to other apartments to fight became the daily grind. It seemed liked all I did at this time was smoke weed and fight. Fighting was fun to me. The adrenaline I get from fighting, plus when I win a fight; to me, that was dominance. Yeah, as I said a few times in the book, every fight wasn't won. Hell, I even got jumped a few times, but that's what gave me a warrior's mindset. It wasn't so much about the loss. So, what if I lost? I made sure I was respected in the end. I made sure everyone knew I wasn't no punk. One of the fights one time turned into a brawl. I ended up getting jumped and my adopted brother James and my other friend—well, at least I thought he was my friend—watched it happen. I know that's fucked-up, right? The worst part is it was their idea to go over there and fight. We had problems with kids in another neighborhood not too far away. I fought one of the kids who was a little older than me. One day he came in my neighborhood to play basketball acting like he was a big shot. He was talking a lot of shit but didn't even live in my complex. Nobody knew who he was or the other kids he was with. There is one thing that you never supposed to do and that's disrespect someone in their own hood. Especially when you not from there. This is another thing that's just not a 'street thing;' it's a 'life thing.' As the saying goes: When in Rome, do as the Romans. He was talking too much, and it led to an argument. One argument led to another, and then a fight broke out. I punched him right in his face while he was standing on the three-point line, and we began fighting. I'm going to be completely honest and will never add details to make me look better. I didn't get my ass beat but I don't feel like I won. I got some good hits in and busted his lip. I feel like I lost because when he slammed me, he could have did a lot of damage. He could have stomped me out or get on top and beat my face in, but everyone that was there broke it up. I didn't get my ass beat, only because it was stopped to avoid that.

After that fight, maybe a week later, James came home one day from the store and said the kid I fought pulled out a weapon on him and was with some other people. He was like he was ready to go over there now and fight. So, we went over there. They were at the basketball court. It immediately becomes a lip wrestling match. James yells out, "I'm back now; what y'all gonna do, now?" The kid who I fought, his sister started arguing back with James. James ended up pulling his pants down and tells her to kiss his ass. I don't know what made him do that; it was weird then and still is weird now. When he did that, her boyfriend automatically rushed towards James, and I rushed jumping in front of James. The boyfriend threw a punch and when he hit me, I'm not going to lie, I knew I made a mistake. It was too late; the fight was started. When I threw my guard up to fight, next thing I know, I was getting punched in the back of my head. After that it was over; it was four-on-one. I hit the ground immediately after getting hit in the back of the head. I was getting kicked and punched. People started calling the police from all the chaos that was going on. People were yelling, "Y'all need to stop!" "Get off of him!" All I could do was cover my face up. When they finally stopped, James helped me up off the ground and we hurried and got out of there before the police got out there. The only thing James could say to me was,

"You would have won that fight if they didn't jump you." At the time I didn't think nothing of it, but I should have beat James's ass. I was too sore; my lip was busted, and my head was hurting. As a kid, you're still learning about the meaning of loyalty and everything that comes with the streets and even life. Then again, I never tried to be anything or anyone tough. I was just me, a kid that didn't care about the consequences. I wasn't acting out for attention. I can honestly say I didn't care.

Things got so bad; my adopted parents got evicted out of the apartment we were living in. It was hard for them to find another apartment because of all the trouble I got into. They got turned down at, like, four other apartments in the area when they tried to move in because I was on the 'No Trespassing' list. They were finally able to find somewhere to move to, but not where they wanted. It was a bad area they were forced to live in. It was exactly where I wanted to be, and it was my type of environment. One of my friends from school lived across the street, so I was happy.

For me Down South, school was the same thing. In Middle School I was a badass kid. I'm sure if you were to ask my teachers about me then, they would tell you I was a lost cause. My second day of school I got in a fight in the lunchroom because I liked this one girl and a boy was talking to her; totally harmless, but I ain't like it. So, I just beat him up to embarrass him. And she could see I am the one she should be talking to. I got kicked out of the school not too long after that. One day, me and the principal's daughter, who was a student at the school, ran away after a parent-teacher conference. We got caught later on that night and all we did was kiss and run through the woods. It just felt so good to be free and do something bad at the same time. I used to love running away. I did that quite a few times in my life. To feel like you escaped whatever bullshit you were dealing with at the time, even if it was just momentarily. It's a feeling I just can't explain. Me and the principal's daughter had to be gone for about two or three hours. We had no plans on returning anytime soon. Until the police picked us up when I was trying to get a free cup of water from a restaurant. That was the last time I saw her or went to that school. Because of that, they sent me to something called 'alternative school.' I didn't last there two weeks. I got into a fight and when the teacher went to break it up, I punched him in the face while he was grabbing me. No, I did not intentionally do that. I just had anger issues. They had police there that put me in handcuffs. I was charged with assault and my foster parents had to sign for me before I could go home. I was put on homeschool and I had to stay home and do my schoolwork. Which was cool with me, but I didn't realize what sort of burden that was on the people around me. My attitude stems from a lot of the earlier trauma I suffered in my life. What was there to care about? I didn't realize then the only thing I was doing was making things worse. I didn't learn that lesson until later in life sometime in my early twenties.

A few weeks later, my foster father's uncle died, so we had to go to Florida for the funeral. I ended up meeting a family I never met before or seen again since then. There was one thing that I encountered on this trip that would change my life forever. I met one of my older cousins who had to be sixteen or seventeen at the time. Me and a bunch of the younger cousins were playing outside, and I see him walk off by himself. My curiosity caused me to follow him. When he caught me following him, he turned and asked me, "What the fuck are you doing, following me?" as he pulled a blunt out his pocket. I asked him if I could smoke with him. He was like, "You don't smoke, little nigga." I replied, "Yeah, I do." He had no idea I hit my first blunt at nine; I was not new to smoking. With hesitation, he passed me the blunt and asked, "Do you wanna see something?" Of course, I said yes. As I'm smoking the weed, he pulls out a gray-and-chrome gun. My eyes lit up wide. I asked him if it was a real gun. He replied, "Let me shoot you with it so you can find out." I laughed as I shook my head no. He started to smile; he could tell I was impressed. He really started to show off. He took the gun and acted like he was aiming it at someone and bragging how good his aim is.

After staring at the gun for a little and obsessing over it, I finally asked him if I could hold it. He looked at me for a few moments and then handed me the gun. I remember the exact feeling I felt when it touched my hand. It was kind of heavy. He immediately told me, "Be careful; it's loaded." When I held the gun, it wasn't my first time seeing a gun. It was my first time holding a gun. While holding the gun all I could think about was, 'what is he doing with it?' Deep down inside I wished it were mine. I didn't know what I would do with a gun, but it would be cool to be eleven with a gun. When I handed it back to him, he was like, "Come on; let's take a walk." He said he wanted to go see his friend. Agreeing to go with him, I walked with him to his friend's house. It was hot as hell in Florida, and it felt like we were walking forever. I think the weed was slowing me down. After the long walk and we finally got to my cousin's friend's house, his friend took one look at me after greeting each other and said to my cousin, "Nigga, you babysitting?" I immediately interjected and shot back, "Hell no; I ain't no fucking baby." They both laughed and then my cousin said, "No, this my little cousin from New York." His friend finally greeted me. My cousin's friend wanted to go play basketball; it was nothing else to really do in this part of Florida. The cool thing about this basketball court, it's where the NBA Legend Tracy McGrady grew up. We went, and we played for a little while. My cousin didn't want to play. So, he sat out. I got no better at basketball from the age of nine to eleven years old when I lost that game to my friend. After a couple games we went back to my cousin's friend's house. My cousin asked his friend if his mom was home. Because he wanted to smoke again, he replied, "No, she will be gone for a little while." We all went to the back yard to get high. While we were smoking, my cousin's friend began telling him about how much money he had saved up from working. It was like five hundred dollars. He was saving up for a car; he had just got his driver's license and my cousin didn't believe him; he was like, "No you don't; you lying. You ain't save up that much." The friend couldn't even tell what was about to happen to him. He didn't see my cousin was baiting him. I didn't even know. I really thought he didn't believe him. His friend ran in the house and grabbed the money to show my cousin and prove his point. He came down with the cash. He pulled out the money, counting and bragging. Then next thing you know; my cousin pulls his gun out. My cousin's friend was shocked; he looked at me to see if it was a joke or something. I just looked down at the ground; it was nothing I could do to help him. I just thought to myself, 'I'm glad I'm not him,' and I was wondering if he was going to shoot him. I didn't know him; at that point in life, I didn't have too many emotions for people I didn't know. When it registered what was going on and he stood no chance, his friend's eyes got so big and watery. You could see the fear in the kid's eyes. All he could say was, "Come on, man, don't do this. Don't do this to me." Begging to my cousin. I was staring in confusion not knowing what was going on. Waiting to see what was going to unfold. There was no way he planned to do this.

His friend was so scared; he was pleading and begging, "Don't shoot me; please don't take my money." The friend ended up giving the money to my cousin, and my cousin told him, "You better not tell nobody or I'm going to shoot you for real." The friend cried out, "I won't!" and we left. We went back to my aunt's house and straight to his room. He hid his gun in his closet. He laughed and counted the money and asked me, "Did you see how scared he was?" I laughed and replied, "Yeah, he was scared." What was I supposed to say or how was I supposed to feel? I didn't know him. All I could wonder was what would have happened if he didn't give up the money. Would he really have shot him? The way he had him crying, how fast he made that money. For a kid like me, that was the wrong thing to show me. That situation is probably what filled in the blank what I could do if I was to ever get a gun. I could make my own money. My cousin gave me fifty dollars and was like, "Don't tell nobody where you got that from." I replied, "I know; I'm not." Lying down that night, all I could think about is what I was going to do with my fifty dollars. I lived down the street from the mall, so chances were I was going to go get a video game from the video game store and a plate of food from the food court. Whatever was left I would have got some weed to smoke for me and my friends. I wanted to see if I could get some more money from him before I leave. At eleven and a half years old, fifty dollars was a lot of money. Even still, I wanted more. The next day was our last day in Florida.

My cousin had to go with his daddy for the day and didn't come back. We left early that morning. Before we left, when no one was watching, while my foster parents were busy loading up the car with oranges and grapefruits they picked off a tree, I remembered where he put the gun. It was at the top of the closet in a sneaker box under some clothes he had folded on top. I knew he couldn't tell on me because he wasn't supposed to have it. I also knew it would be a while before we seen each other again. If we ever seen each other again and even if we did, I wasn't scared if I had to fight him. I knew this would be the perfect moment; no one was watching. I went into his room with my toy bag like I was getting all my things together and creeped over to his closet. I saw exactly where he put it the day before. When I grabbed the gun, I had to admire it for a minute. The shine to it made me want to take it more. I'll never forget the feeling; I knew I had to have it. I put the gun in my toy bag and didn't think twice. He'd left ten dollars on the dresser, and I took that too.

I moved fast because I did not want to get caught. My excitement made me anxious. I wanted to do what I saw my cousin do. I wanted to make someone cry and feel pain. I was so young and ignorant at the time. All I wanted to do was scare people and make them fear me. Money was the last thing on my mind. I wanted someone to fear me the same way I seen my cousin had that kid fear him. I knew what pain felt like. It was time I stopped receiving it and start giving it. That had become my mindset. I hurried outside and put my bag all the way in the third row of the minivan and rode all the way back to South Carolina. Every chance I got in the back seat I looked at it. I would put my hand in the bag to hold it. I thought about all the things I could do with the gun. When I got back to South Carolina, I couldn't wait to do what I saw my cousin do to his friend. Have someone fear me. I felt like I could do that. I knew I could. By eleven, I already knew whatever you did when you go outside, don't be weak. People always had jokes and picked on the weak ones. The weak ones often got bullied.

We pulled up to the house. I helped unload the stuff out the car. I grabbed an orange to snack on and I put the gun on my hip and went outside to show my friends what I got from Florida. On the way to show them what I just got, I seen an opportunity. An opportunity to show I can be just as vicious as my cousin. A chance to prove I'm far from weak. I saw this kid that lived two buildings down from me who I fought at the park a while back. I ran up to him, looked at him and pulled the gun out. Just like my cousin did and just like I saw in movies. I cocked it back to scare him and I could tell he was afraid. I smiled and lowered the gun; as I lowered the gun, I accidentally hit the trigger. POW! The bullet shot through a window, and I ran like I've never ran before in my life.

I ran through a path that had a tunnel. Behind the apartment complex I lived in was an elementary school and two more apartment complexes that were nicer next to a pond with a tunnel that led to a shopping center and a mall across the street. I ran through the cut that led to the tunnel. I hid the gun on the other side of the tunnel. I dug a hole next to the tree that had an orange band tied around it. I picked that tree so I wouldn't forget where it was at. After I hid the gun, I went straight to the mall, which wasn't far from where I hid the gun. The mall was my favorite place to go, especially when I used to meet up with this girl I liked. All we used to do was walk around the mall for hours going in and out of stores, talking, playing, and even kissed a few times. Me and her are actually still friends to this day. On this particular afternoon though, I was there by myself. I heard the sirens going to where the gunshot was at, when I was entering the mall. My plan was to hide out at the mall until I felt like things were good and I would head back in the house. I walked around the mall and went into the food court and ate the free samples. After a couple hours, the mall was closing so I had to leave. I went back to the spot I left my gun. As I headed home, I knew I had to be swift and move with precautions. It was three different ways to enter my apartment complex. I thought I took the entrance I was less likely to get caught at. I was dead wrong; the police were waiting. As I was passing the mailbox, a police officer drove past me and turned around and hit the lights. Two more cars swarmed in. They jumped out with their guns drawn. That was only the third time in my life a gun was pulled out on me at this point in my life. Two times were the police. The third, me and a group of friends were shot at. The first time was at my grandmother's house and the FBI was looking for my cousin Kevin. Kevin was my cousin on my adopted mother's side. I used to look up to him, too, growing up. He was a true hustler and kept big money in his pockets. It was Father's Day. The FBI surrounded my grandmother's house; they were in the woods in the back yard, and they were on the side of the house. They must have thought that would be the best time to catch him. They came into the room with the kids, with their guns drawn and made us put our hands up. Walked us in the dining room and made us put our heads down. Me, I kept peaking and was watching them go through the house. Once again, this was a moment I should have learned from a situation; instead, I normalized that going to jail is a thing that comes with the lifestyle. I heard a lot of stories from the older guys and even saw a few people go to jail. It was something I was not afraid of happening.

Being surrounded this time was much different. I was the one they wanted. As my hands were up, the black cop who was approaching me was shouting, "Don't move!" Then another one moved slowly behind him. When he got to me, he patted me down and took the gun off my hip and the other cop cuffed me. By then it seemed like half the neighborhood was outside. Even the boy and his mama. She started yelling, "Take his little badass to jail. He could have killed my son." They took me to the house first to talk to my parents. The cop said to me, "Do you know you could have lost your life?" He told me they would have shot me if I would have made any sudden move. I just shrugged my shoulders. To be honest, at this point in my life I didn't care about much. I was thinking to myself, 'I would be better off dead anyway; at least I wouldn't be hurting.' My adopted mother quickly pointed out that I didn't care. Like she was reading my mind. She let him know I never do; I think everything is funny. She also made him aware I had a court date coming up for assaulting a teacher. The cop told them they should whip my ass more. My parents begin telling him how they adopted me and how out of control I am. How I run away frequently and like staying out all night. I'm disrespectful and how bad I am in school. They all agreed and said I was unappreciative and that I needed to be locked up in a juvenile facility. Most people growing up looked at it like at least someone is trying to give you some of the things you never had. The thing about that is they never understood that the things I never had is what made me feel so empty. He told them it's ok; they wouldn't have to worry about me for a little bit. I was going with them to the department of juvenile justice. He told them if I stay on the route that I'm on I would be dead or in jail by the time I was eighteen. They took me off and I would stay in juvenile detention for the next two years of my life. I was gone for the rest of my middle school years. After I got out, I was in high school. As you are learning, I was coming off the sidewalk and getting involved in the streets.

Chapter 5

Normalizing the Pain

Everyone's got the answers, but no one wants to solve the problem. When you deal with pain and trauma over a long period of time, do you ever heal? After a while you just begin to cope with it; you don't see it as anything but normal. You learn how to function over time. When I say you learn how to function, you function in what you believe to be reality. You begin to believe the pain is normal. Eventually, you get tired of being the one getting hurt, and you become the one inflicting pain.

People get in the streets for all sorts of reasons. Some do it because they think it's easier, some do it because they think it's cool, and some do it because they were forced into it and didn't have another way. Some of us, this was all we saw, and this was all we knew.

When I first got to the juvenile detention center, the guard tried to scare me. "Ain't no mommy and daddy in here; you on your own, boy," I looked him dead in his eyes and told him, "I never had any parents anyway." The things I think that judge was trying to teach me by sending me there did not work. It actually did the exact opposite. I learned who I wasn't going to be while I was there. I was never going to be the type to get pushed around. I wasn't going to be weak. It was really no difference for me. I was used to having to adapt to different environments. I didn't have anything to miss. I didn't have anything to lose. I was always bounced around anyway, growing up in foster care.

So, for them two years, the only thing it did was help create the beast. I learned how to be a wolf. I learned how to survive early. I learned to survive on my own.

At first when I got there, one of the older kids took me under his wing. In this dorm, he was the man. I started rolling with his gang. One day, after getting out the shower, I headed back to my room, and I see all my stuff is missing out my locker that they give all the juveniles to hold their belongings. Someone had took the toothpaste and spread "Fuck you, New York" on my locker. New York, that's what everyone called me in there.

So, I need to back up a bit. Before that happened to me, I saw a similar situation and the person whose stuff got taken would start saying a lot of disrespectful things to get the person mad enough to admit they did it. I went to the middle of the wing, and I yelled out, "Whoever did this is a bitch… Fuck you, your mama, your daddy, and your grandma! I hope they die of AIDS!" That's when I heard, "What the fuck you say?" That's when I repeated it in a much louder tone. This tall kid, who rolled with the one who looked out for me, was like, "Say that shit to me in the bathroom." The bathroom is where we would fight so we didn't get a write-up and have to go into lockup. When we got in the bathroom, I could see he was angry. Come to find out, his grandmother died a few months before I said that. I touched a weak spot for him. Which was what I was trying to do anyway. He threw the first punch, and we begin fighting. The way he threw that punch, you can tell he was trying to knock my head off. He missed with the first swing. I weaved the punch and quickly threw two punches to counter his miss. I landed both hits. For a minute it even looked like I was winning. I was throwing good punches and landing them. He grabbed me and we locked up. While we were holding onto each other, both of us were trying not to get slammed. Then all of a sudden, I started getting punched from everywhere; I was up against more than two fists before I realized it. It became six-on-one pretty fast. At first, I was still trying to fight a little bit, then I hit the ground. I started getting kicked; all I could do was ball up. I got to look and the kid I thought was like 'big bro' was one of the ones whipping my ass.

Yo! Until this point in life, that was my first time ever being betrayed like that. Especially by someone I thought was my friend. I had no idea what made him do that or why he didn't like me. It did something to me that would affect me forever. The black eye healed, the swollen lip went down, and the bruises went away. That feeling of being betrayed takes a while to go away. In fact, it never leaves. The scars from it always remain. Getting through the juvenile detention center and spending two years there, I would compare it to a person going to basic training and becoming a soldier. Except the wars and battles I was preparing for wasn't overseas and you weren't getting no medal when it was over. If you were lucky to still be standing.

Once I returned home after being gone for two years, it was weird at first. I was a teenager, now a freshman in high school, and my adopted parents moved to the suburbs. I went from being in predominantly black hoods to moving to a mostly-white suburban area. It was a cultural shock. The first few months I did okay. I was mostly bad in school, but nothing too crazy yet. I played football, so that kept me kind of busy and out of trouble for a little. That didn't last long. The saying was true for me. You can take me out the hood but couldn't take the hood out of me.

When I got out to the suburbs, it was a coincidence that two of the brothers I was locked up with in the dorm at the juvenile detention center ended up living out there in the same area. My boy Bubba and his little brother. I also met my boy who grew to be my best friend and brother Tony aka T-mac living out there. Me and T-mac connected on another level: he was adopted; I was adopted. We somewhat understood each other's path. We clicked instantly the first day I met him. He introduced himself to me as the Mack of all Macks. Which I thought was funny. We started talking about girls and the rest was history; we were together every day after that. When me and Bubba ended up linking back up, it was all love there too. Bubba was released from there almost a year after me. He got released 2007; I got released 2006. It was good to have them around. It was like having actual brothers. We got in trouble together and we fought together. We all knew what it was like to be locked up, so none of us was scared. We were some badass teenagers. Well, I wouldn't call us bad; I'll rather say, 'misguided teens.'

Being around my homies was an escape. It was a lot better than being home. I hated being at that house. Being there I began to become filled with hatred. The hate grew so much I began hating my own life. Especially after my adopted father stabbed me during a fight with a pair of scissors and I went back away to juvenile detention for forty-five days. I was fourteen at the time. It was the beginning of the summer after my freshman year in school. I'll go into more details about that later in the chapter.

Me and my adopted father did not get along; we barely spoke. If you ask me anything about anything we ever talked about, I can't recall a conversation we had. I can't even tell you a lesson he taught me in life. It was like I didn't have a father. In which reality I didn't. Him and his son relationship was decent; it was better than ours.

What I can say about him, he did work his ass off, though. Now I'm going to tell you about the time he stabbed me and why I feel the way I feel about him.

I was on the computer on MySpace, a social media site that was famous before Facebook. I was messaging my girlfriend at the time who lived across town from me. He walked upstairs and got mad I was on the computer and playing music. He hated rap music. Plus he probably felt I could listen to that in my room. Which I couldn't, because I only had a radio. On the computer I could play the songs I wanted to hear. I will never forget, I was listening to Lil Wayne's "Da Drought 3." I was in such a good mood. He said to me, "Turn that nonsense off." I told him it wasn't nonsense; he was killing it, and that it was better than the music he listens to. Then he went on a rant about how 'it's his house.' I just got tired of hearing it. Like I said, we really didn't get along. So, I replied, "I don't care who house it is, but just take the computer." He said, "What you said to me?" By this time, I'm out the room the computer is in. I'm in my room which is right next to the computer room. He mumbled a couple curse words and rushed towards me and grabbed me with one hand and punched me.

I just started swinging back and hitting him in the face. I threw three punches; the first two he ate, but I know he felt that third one. I saw it in his eyes when they got big. All that did was make him madder. He slammed me with ease because he was twice my weight. He weighed three-something and I probably was one hundred twenty-five pounds soaking wet. When he slammed me, he grabbed the scissors off my dresser and was on top of me. I saw his hand come down, but I couldn't stop it because he was stronger than me. He stabbed me in the neck by my collar bone. I kept moving, trying to get him off me. It was like I was swinging for my life. He stabbed me again. He got me in the chest. I was wiggling, then he went to stab me one more time before my adopted mother broke it up. He got me on the side. Luckily, it was the dull kid scissors that they have in elementary schools. I probably would be dead. That shit burned. It hurt not only physically, but mentally and emotionally.

I wondered, 'why would you try to kill me? I'm supposed to be your son.' After the fight, I ran to where Bubba was staying with a girl he was messing with at the time. It was in the neighborhood right by mine. Really all I had to do was go through the path in the woods and it was right there. I banged on the door. Bubba's girlfriend's mother answered the door like, "Who the hell is banging on my door like that?" She answered the door and immediately called her daughter and Bubba. Bubba looked at me and was furious that that happened to me. His girl's mother doctored me up. When she was done, Bubba was like, "Fuck that; let's go over there and get him back. Ain't nobody about to do you like that." Bubba don't play about me or any of his brothers. When we went back over to my house, there was three police cars in the driveway. So, we left. I did not go back home. The police began looking for me for assault and battery and running away from home. That had me furious; I couldn't understand how he didn't get in no trouble. I mean, I'm the minor and I'm the one who got stabbed. I stayed away, and I hid out at a friend house, then went to my girlfriend's house. The one I told you about earlier in the chapter that stayed across town from me. Bubba's house was too close to mine for me to hide out. His house was in the same neighborhood as the girl he was talking to. I knew they would be looking for me in that neighborhood.

I stayed on the run for a few weeks; two, to be exact. I had two girls helping me and a couple older guys I knew that I met in the streets. I always hung out with people older than me. When I'm saying older, I mean sixteen, seventeen, and eighteen years old. To be frankly honest, now that I think about it, I'm glad I was caught because that same day I was caught I was going to throw my life away. I never got over the fact that this man stabbed me and tried to take my life. It wasn't the first time he hurt me.

He broke my tooth one time when he punched me in the mouth for talking back, when I was younger. Yes, I had a couple extra dentist appointments to get my teeth fixed while growing up. Another time when I was nine years old, I had to have laser eye surgery. I went outside to ride my bike. I didn't have permission to go outside but I figured I wouldn't get in trouble if I didn't leave the yard. I was dead wrong. I was riding my bike in the driveway. I was coming back towards him because he was yelling at me for being outside. I told him I didn't know I couldn't be in the driveway. Then bam! He threw an ice scraper at me, and it hit me dead in the eye. Next thing I know, I couldn't see. My vision was blurry. That's why him stabbing me made me hate his guts. I wanted him dead at that time.

A friend was going to let me hold one of his guns, but I had to get dropped off to him. I didn't tell him all the details; I only told him was that I was going to get the person back that stabbed me. The girl's house I was staying at, her daddy was a truck driver. He would only be home two weekends a month and he happened to be home this weekend. He didn't like me too much. I was not good enough for his daughter. Now that I'm a father with daughters, I don't blame him. You only want the best for your children. Especially your daughters. I was using her phone calling everybody for a ride. Her dad asked why I just don't go home. He wasn't too fond of me being over there; he didn't know what was going on. He definitely didn't like it. I was on the phone, so I hurried outside to avoid the question. I was outside when she began telling him what was going on and that it was okay because her mom said it was. About an hour later her dad walked up to me and asked me where I was going. I told him I needed to go to a friend's house for some cash and I'll probably stay over there. Making sure I left out my plans about getting the gun and getting revenge on my adopted father for stabbing me. He offered to take me over there. Not thinking twice and not having no other options, I needed the ride, so, I accepted it. On the way he told me he was hungry and was going to get me something to eat. We pulled up to a fast-food restaurant named Hardee's. He told me to wait in the car while he goes in and gets the food. He asked me what I wanted. I told him it didn't matter. I wasn't really that hungry; I was anxious thinking about what I was planning to do. When he walked in, after about ten or fifteen minutes, two police cars pulled in and blocked his car in.

They made me step out of the car and they put the handcuffs on me. Her dad finally walked out of the restaurant with no food in his hands saying, "Sorry, I had to do what was best for you." He went over and talked to the police, and they took me away. I didn't really understand why he said he was doing what was best for me because on the way there he really seemed like he was about to help me, like he cared. Even told me stories to try to relate to me. He even told me if I ever needed him, he would be there for me. I guess that's one of the reasons why my trust is so messed up in people. Like I stated earlier, I only did forty-five days in juvenile detention and got sent home with probation afterwards.

I was arrested for running away and for the assault, which was bullshit. He should have went to jail for stabbing a minor. To all the younger ones that read that story: I didn't understand it then why I only went to jail. The reason I went to jail was because of my terrible reputation and many run-ins with the law. If you build a certain reputation, it follows you even when you're in the right; everyone is still going to look at you like you're wrong because that's what you're known to do. For us and people like me, you're guilty until proven innocent. I ran into that a lot in my life. So, after getting out that time, I really didn't want to go back to my adopted parents' house, but I didn't have a choice. With school starting, I did not want to go back. I was deeply depressed, and I really started to question my existence. I didn't understand what was my purpose. What was the whole purpose of my life? I had no mama, no daddy, no family, and the family I did have barely even liked me. My other cousins grew a strong dislike because they felt I was ungrateful and disrespecting their family. My foster father stabbed me. I always felt like I didn't belong anywhere. I always asked myself why.

'Why' is a question I have been asking myself since I can remember. Why am I here? Why does this keep happening to me? Why doesn't it get any better?

Why can't things go the way I planned? Or why did I have to grow up in foster care? Why would my mama smoke crack with me in her stomach? Why did I never get to meet my mother or father? Why? Why? Why? And I'm usually just left with the question and not the answer. See, I can ask myself all I want, I can make up answers too, do research, read case studies on other kids who went through what I did and form a slightly accurate opinion, but it'll never be fact. I'll never get the answer I need.

I remember after getting out, it was like a dark cloud was over me. I had a lot of hate and anger built up. I was still fourteen years old. My fifteenth birthday was approaching in a couple months. It was a hot night, but the feeling was cold. I just felt like I had enough with life. I was tired of the unanswered questions, I was tired of feeling like I was alone in the world, and I was tired of feeling like I don't belong. A few weeks prior to that night, one of my older friends told me to hold a gun for him. As you can see, through my childhood, guns were easily accessible for me. I agreed to hold the gun for him. On this night, I just was tired of living. I didn't care. I never really cared about much at that point. Not life, not sports, not school, and not my grades. My grades in school were good without even applying myself, but I didn't care enough to try. On this night I was sitting in my room at my adopted parents' house. The house was beautiful. They worked hard to get out the hood, and with a little government assistance they moved to the suburbs where they had been for maybe two years. I was there maybe a year at that moment.

This night I was sitting in the dark just staring at the posters on my wall, and a cold feeling hit me and my chest got tight. All I could think about in that moment was, 'Why am I here? I'm tired of the pain!' Waking up just to feel the same pain and worries, I had enough. I also felt like I wasn't good enough that my own mama didn't even want me. Thinking of all the abuse I had to endure through the years. I just had enough. So, I went in the closet, and under the clothes was two book bags. One was for school, and one had the gun in it. I grabbed the gun out, I locked my room door, and I went to sit on the bed. I was crying as I was just staring at the gun. In my mind I knew no one would miss me. After staring at the gun long enough, I turned the gun toward me and began looking at the barrel. Me and the barrel must have had a staredown for maybe five minutes, but it felt so much longer. While I was staring down that barrel, I remember the 50-Cent lyric playing in my head, "death got too easy because life is hard." Agreeing with every word of those lyrics I was ready to throw my hand in because the cards life dealt me felt impossible to play. So, I put the gun to my head, took a deep breath, and closed my eyes. I put my left index finger on the trigger and began counting down in my head. I get down to one and take a deep breath and start over. This time I'm counting slower, 'five … four … three … two …'so when I finally get to one, I just pull the trigger. "Click-Click." I open my eyes, confused why the gun didn't go off, so, I put the gun back in the closet. I just stared at the ceiling. It wouldn't be my last suicide attempt in my life. After that failed attempt, I still felt funny, like things were still wrong.

Nightmares at night made it hard to go to sleep. Some nights I would have nightmares about me dying or things I have seen or some of the abuse I received over the years. I would have nightmares about me being in prison. The one I hated the most growing up was when I was being chased. I would get chased all over the place and get caught and I couldn't do nothing to help myself. I was helpless. It was bad; I had to sleep with the radio on and rap or sing myself to sleep or even talk on the phone until I fell asleep. I've been prescribed medicine for it and to help me sleep. It just was hard to sleep. Even as an adult now, I still have trouble falling to sleep. Gladly, I don't have no more dreams about being killed or being in prison.

Entering the tenth grade, I was in a whole different mindset. I was more about making money. I was into fashion, and I was definitely trying to impress the girls. I used to hate the cheap clothes my foster parents bought me. Now that I'm older and a parent, I understand being a parent is not easy. Plus, they were older parents. They didn't know anything about fashion. Luckily, I could fight good, so I wasn't getting picked on like other kids whose clothes weren't up to par. To make money at this point, there weren't a lot of options. I would sell the medication I was on; I was prescribed Adderall, so I would sell those. The kids at that school loved those. I would also sell a little bit of weed or do burglaries. I would have rather sold something than take it. But I didn't mind doing either.

The 'by any means necessary' mindset took effect. After a while, I began getting a little money. I was able to buy my own phone with free minutes after 9:00. Which was huge; I was able to talk to the girls when I want. Having a cell phone for a kid in 2007 was huge; it's nothing like it is today. My ten-year-old has a phone, so it's not as big of a deal as it was then.

Soon enough, I was kicked out of school. They had enough of suspending me. They were ready to get me out of there for good. I had too many fights and write-ups. Then when someone snitched on me about selling pills in school, and they didn't catch me with them, it really made it a mission for the assistant principal. Luckily, I had a feeling and knew what was about to happen before it did. That day the assistant principal walked to my class with a police officer and told me to come to the office with my book bag. I was in biology class. First, they talked to the teacher in the hallway. While the assistant principal was doing that, I put the pills in a textbook, and I put the book on a kid's desk I used to sell them to and was cool with. When I got to the office, I walked in with my head up, keeping calm like I did no wrong. They searched me, they searched my bookbag, and they searched my locker. I never used my locker or even remembered the combination to it. So, I knew it was nothing in there. Only thing they found was a Swisher Sweet I had in my bookbag to smoke weed in after school. They expelled me from school for bringing tobacco on school property.

Two months later I was back in the juvenile detention center for a burglary and marijuana charges. While going to court in the back of the transport van, I told one of the boys who got caught with me to call Bubba and tell Bubba to tell my adopted brother, James, to give him the weed that was under the sink before they find it. When the detective came and got me, I was walking down the steps and seen him and turned around. I went grabbed the weed and put it in a towel and threw it under the bathroom sink.

Therefore, earlier in the book, I said I don't really look at James like a brother because he never treated me like one. James snitched that I had two ounces of weed under the bathroom sink. He turned the weed in to his parents and they told the detective. One day the detective came for a visit. The JCO came in my unit and pulled me out my unit. For those that don't know, a JCO is a Juvenile Correctional Officer. On the visit, the detective informed me he filed new charges besides the Burglary 2nd Degree. I was also getting a PWID. Possession With Intent to Distribute marijuana. He tried to get me to tell where I got the weed from, but I was not doing that. I didn't talk to him before I knew not to talk to him now. There is one rule in the streets I learned very early, and it gets installed into most kids in the urban community. Never snitch. Don't be a tattletale. No ratting— however you want to put it. I honored that code with everything in me.

While I was gone and locked up, James sold all my things I bought. My PlayStation 3, my DVDs, he even sold some of my sneakers. Then was bragging he put me in jail because I'm not his brother. We weren't close, but it still kind of hurt. I used to take up for him and fight his battles because he was too scared to fight. I even fought my best friend Bubba one day because he was picking on him, and my foster brother didn't want to fight. So, him doing that killed any chance of us ever having a relationship. I did almost fifteen months in juvenile detention and came home on juvenile parole.

This was another defining moment in my life. I was fifteen years old; I had no one to talk to, so I started writing. Writing was my escape. My escape from the pain and everything going on around me. Writing was a way to gather my thoughts together. I wrote poems and started writing about my life. I started to think about the things I went through in life. I felt like people should know my pain and why I am the way I am. I told myself and everyone I communicated with, I was going to write me a book. I wanted to write a book about the things that went on in my life. So, I started to write. I completed two chapters and never finished. Because of the way I wrote, the director at the facility thought I was special and talented. He chose me to give a speech in front of different politicians. On the day of the speech, I got treated like royalty and I got to eat food that wasn't State-issued food. They separated me and put me in a classroom. They had me put a suit on and took pictures. One of the teachers who was watching me went over the speech with me. After the rehearsal she started asking me questions about my background and upbringings.

Those questions usually made me uncomfortable because I didn't have the answers. So, in the process of me telling her about the things I did know, she asked did I want answers to the questions I didn't know. She told me even though my parents were dead, I can still call the hospital I was born at and get some information. She let me use her cell phone even though she wasn't supposed to, and I called Harlem Hospital. Then it happened. I gave them my name and the lady on the phone read me my parents' names. I knew my dad's name because I was named after him. I didn't know my mom's name. When the lady said it, I was filled with so many emotions. Mostly even more pain because I couldn't put a face to the name. One answer gave me fifty more questions. I was released six months after that.

Getting out this time, things were different this time around. I was sixteen. I felt like I was a man. My adopted father was in his last month of life when I had got out. He was diagnosed with stage four cancer while I was still locked up; I didn't even know. He died exactly a month after I was released. We never really got along. I can probably count the number of conversations we had from the time I was young until his death. On July 2, 2009, I saw him take his last breath. I can't say I was sad; that would be a lie. To me it was what it was; it was a part of life and just his time to go. I really didn't have any emotions about his death. A big piece of me was thankful for him though, and before he took his last breath, I did get to tell him, "Thank you for everything." At the end of the day, my life was what it was, it was pretty fucked-up, but it could have also been way worse, and it wasn't, because of him.

We didn't have much of a relationship. Like I said, I can't even tell you any conversations we had because we only ever had small talk. He wasn't someone I could get advice from or even go to about my problems or feelings. To be honest, he never even took the time to get to know me as his son. That still didn't stop me from appreciating the idea he had to change another kid's life who wasn't his. Even if he didn't do the best job, he still took on the task. It was just no way I could be sad about his passing because it's hard to feel pain when it has already been normalized.

Chapter 6

Nightmares from the Bottom

Have you ever gone to sleep and seen the same thing for several nights in a row? The same dream or image every night? That's how it was after the first time I ever saw someone get killed. I was nine years old. The day started off so regularly, no way of knowin' what was gonna go down. I went up the block to a friend's house and I will never forget it. He opened the door and he started calling me trash in basketball. I immediately shot back at him. "Yeah, right, nigga; I'm the next A.I." Referring to Allen Iverson, who was my favorite basketball player at the time. I knew I was lying. Truth is, I was terrible at basketball. I just could never let nobody tell me how good I wasn't. It was up to me to determine that. I said to him, "Let's ride our bikes and go hoop. I'll play you for five dollars and some Pokémon cards." He told me he had to go grab something from the corner store for his grandmother, but I was on for the challenge.

We raced our bikes to the store and rode back with me coming in second place. That was one loss already; I needed to school this chump in the basketball game. All I hear coming from the front is, "You slow-ass nigga and you think you can beat me at ball." When we got back to the house, my boy grabbed his ball and threw it to me to hold onto. We got to the court and there were two other games going on at the time. We went to the empty court and began shooting around. Then it was game time. Neither one of us was ball players, but we loved basketball. We could barely put up a three-pointer, we were so young. He started winning. He began talking crazy about how bad I suck and how I can't shoot. That only made me madder, and I tried to play harder. I thought maybe I'd warm up and my shots would start falling. The ball just wouldn't go in for me. The game wasn't looking like it was going to go my way. Then an argument broke out. Next thing we hear someone yell is, "Foul, bitch!" Then, "That wasn't no foul, nigga," the other guy replied. Then he must have thought about the insult thrown at him. "Who are you calling a bitch?" They started arguing and insulting each other. Then they started fighting. The guys that they were playing with broke up the fight and sent away the one who threw the first punch.

All the chaos seemed like it was over at that point, but that's not how the streets go. Me and my homie got back to playing ball. He beat me in the first game, so I wanted another shot, best two out of three, and soon enough we were in the middle of the second game. The next thing you know, shots rang out. Everyone that was in the park ran like roaches when the lights come on. Shootings like that happened pretty often. Not every day or every minute, but enough to where the people in my hood knew exactly what to do when the metal started flying. You can become so accustomed to the shots, you don't even always run, and it don't startle you. After the shots stopped, I started to hear screams. After finally being able to walk after being frozen by fear, I see the shirtless man lying there, bleeding from his chest and stomach. A few people were yelling his name telling him to fight, to stay awake as they put pressure on his wounds. Me and my friend just stood there watching the blood pour out this guy we just shared the court with not two minutes ago. Eventually, some girl and guy walked over to us and told us to get out of there, that this ain't shit we supposed to be seeing.

They were right. I was traumatized. I never heard anything about that shooting after that, but I'm guessing the guy died there on the court. I couldn't sleep for a couple nights because of what I saw. In my nightmare it was me that was shot. Except nobody cared. It was like I didn't even exist. Everybody kept walking past me as I bled out and cried for help. I was nine years old at that time.

I learned as I got older you don't always got to be asleep to see a nightmare. Nightmares when you sleep is one thing. You can wake up from those. What about the ones you wish you could wake up from but it's actually reality and you not sleeping? As a kid, how do you function normal by society standards? How do you pay attention in school? How do you not act out? I made it out of foster care; technically speaking, I was adopted. There are kids, though, who aren't as fortunate as I was. They age out and become grown without ever having no family, not even a dysfunctional one.

There is a statistic that say 20 percent of the kids in foster care will become homeless. Can you imagine the number of kids that is in a big city like New York, Los Angles, Chicago, or any other major city in America? According to kids-alliance.org, 75 percent of students in foster care are performing below grade level. Most of the kids are labeled trouble and only have one place for them to turn to, and that is the streets. That's the motivation for a kid to join a gang. It gives you a family. It gives the ones who need protection just that. It makes you feel like you a part of something. The gang life gives you something you feel like you don't have. It feels good to feel like you a part of something. Me personally, when I was younger, I did the same thing. I wanted to be a part of something too. I would run with a gang, that was, until one of the homies killed the other homie over a female. After that I quickly realized that it isn't what it's made out to be. Being in a gang doesn't guarantee the ones you are rolling with will remain loyal. I seen a lot of disloyalty between people in the same gang, same set. Plus I knew staying neutral would be more profitable for me. I didn't have limitations on what neighborhood I could go into or what side of town I shouldn't go to. I decided I would ride for whoever rode for me. I didn't care about any color or none of that no more. Most of my friends today are in gangs. Some are Bloods, some are Crips, and some are GDs. I always got their back; I just don't get involved in the gang beefs. There are a lot of misunderstandings people have about that lifestyle. I'm not going to touch on that in this book. There are plenty of books that do. It's a harsh reality, but it's reality.

Look at me after my adopted father died on July 2, 2009. I was sixteen at the time he died. You would think me and my adopted mother would get closer. That did not happen. In fact, it was the complete opposite. We were never close, but we grew even further apart. I can't say it was all her fault we weren't close. It was times growing up she tried to be there for me. It was times she tried to love me. There were times she would look me in my face and ask me, "What's wrong?" Trying to get through to me and trying to get me to talk. I mostly shut her out. I didn't want the hugs; I didn't want to talk. In my opinion, she eventually kind of gave up. To me, she loved me, but not like she loved James. She loved him on another level; it was like James could do no wrong. A piece of me also understood that was her birth son. Other things played a part in our strenuous relationship too. For instance, my adopted mother hated the friends I would choose. To her, they were thugs up to no good. To me, those were my brothers; they always had my back even when she didn't. I could never turn my back on them. She hated the decisions I made. Now I know, as a man, she only wanted what she thought was best for me. We also used to beef a lot about the fact I always had different girls at her house having sex. I mean she really hated that. I guess it was against her religion. I was sixteen years old; all I thought about was sex. I was not no ugly kid. I never had trouble with the girls.

While I was locked up in the juvenile detention center, James ended up catching a case for burglary. He was sentenced a few months after I came home. He didn't have to do much time because, of course, he told on everyone who committed the crime with him. James is the perfect example of what happens when guys try to pretend to be something they are not. He was so scared; he told the detectives about crimes they did and got away with. He only did ninety days in prison in a shock boot camp. Well, I shouldn't say "only" ninety days, because a day in jail is one day too many, to be honest. What I'm saying is, for the crime he should have did more time, but he took the weak way out and told.

I know many people reading this say they would tell, too. They are not going to go down by their self. Listen to my theory; when you get into the streets you know what you sign up for. It comes with certain consequences if you get caught doing certain actions. Once you agree to them terms, you're supposed to honor that. It's like an unwritten contract. My personal opinion: if you get caught as a man, you should have honor; you accept your consequences, take whatever comes with that, and deal with it. You knew when you did that crime, whatever it was, there was a chance you would get caught. Why bring the next person down because you don't want to deal with that consequence alone? It was your choice; you didn't have to do that crime. Also, let's be honest: there is a code to everything, every group, every brotherhood; no snitching is not just a street thing. Yeah, society wants people to believe that, but why the bad cops don't rat out the other bad cops?

Say what you will about the life of crime, being a rat is worse. No, I don't think it's snitching if you tell the police and you're not in the streets. Then you owe no one loyalty, and you are a tax-paying citizen who has every right to call the cops. The last line was strictly for the ones who are in the streets.

Around the same time, my best friend T-mac ended up catching a ten-year bid for armed robbery. He ended up robbing the pizza man and the pizza man shot him. Everyone tried to stop him from doing it, but once a person is determined to do something it's almost impossible to save them from themself. Now with my best friend gone, I kind of branched out and started doing my own thing on another side of town. As the new guy on the block, you have to prove yourself. Which did not take me long to do. You can choose to be a wolf or a sheep. It comes with two different mentalities. The wolf is the hunter. The sheep gets hunted. I damn sure wasn't going to let anyone prey on me. My first chance would come when I began beefing with one of the guys who lived out there. Big boy thought he was tough, and the situation ended up earning me a lot of respect because it showed. I wasn't scared and would take it to any level it needed to go to.

I had stopped at an Exxon gas station one late night coming back from a girl's house. I really didn't need to stop. I was on a quarter-tank of gas, but I wanted to roll up and my friend I was with at the time didn't know how to roll up. So, I decided I would just kill two birds with one stone. It was a few days, maybe a week, after me and this guy's brother fought at the mall. He pulled his car up not too far from where my homeboy was pumping my gas. I was in the driver seat. He yelled out, "So you think you hard pussy run up on me like that? You lucky." I was looking at my phone at the time, responding to a text. I immediately was shocked, and if he had a gun, I would have been dead that day or shot because I did not see him. I yelled back at him, "Yeah, step out the car; I'll beat your ass just like I did your brother." He threatened me and said he definitely going to see me again and see if I'm still talking. He sped off and got caught at the light. Still upset about the interaction we just had. I told my homeboy, "Hurry up and you drive." I told him to follow him. I had a tan Chevy Malibu at the time. I was only seventeen; it was my first car. I jumped on the passenger side, and I said, "Fuck that; I'm tired of this nigga, and he threatened me." Without thinking twice, when we made the left, he sped up again. My homeboy sped up behind him. I cocked my homeboy's 9mm Smith and Wesson back and just started letting off shots in his direction. I let off four shots. He swerved left, then right, trying to dodge the bullets, and turned in a neighborhood. One bullet hit the taillight; the other one hit the trunk. We kept going. I wanted to follow, but my homeboy was like, "No, the police is gonna be on the way soon." So, he kept going to flee the scene. I told one of the other homies what happened, and we were all ready to put this beef to an end for good. So, me and a few of my homies pulled up to his house. Luckily, he wasn't home. I was mad when I shot at him, and the bullet didn't hit him. I always had anger issues.

I hated being provoked or bothered. Especially if I didn't do nothing to you. I wasn't the one that started this beef, but I wanted to end it. Come to find out, he started beefing with me over a girl. A girl, let's just say, that got around and was already messing with a lot of other guys besides me and him. I guess he loved her. I felt like he came for me because I was the new guy. Of course, the police came straight for me, but I knew they couldn't prove it was me just because we didn't like each other, so they questioned me. The police tried to scare me into telling on myself. I knew better and that they didn't have any real information, so they had to let me go. I stopped going out to that neighborhood after that situation. Situations like that do give your ego a stroke. I knew I could become a beast; I knew I could bring the fear out of people.

I needed to make some money; I started thinking of ways to get money fast. I knew it was no easier way than robbing or doing burglaries. I started plotting, then I began robbing a lot. I would never hit big; usually the people I was sticking up or kicking their doors didn't have much, but that didn't matter. The most I probably got was from a few hundred dollars up to a thousand dollars and some drugs and guns. One trip out of town and luck on our side changed everything for me and few of my friends. Because of statute of limitations, I can't go into exact details, but let's just say we ended up with almost six figures split four ways. I ran through that money so fast it was hard to imagine I ever had it and that money brought me a lot of problems and hate. We were in the malls buying everything we had wanted. I was seventeen, getting into clubs and strip clubs. I was in the VIP partying with rappers. There was nothing you could tell me at the time.

One of the guys I rolled with at this time was hated, I felt like, by everyone, but a few people feared him, so they did nothing to him. I really thought I was untouchable until they tried to kill us at the club one night and ended up shooting a girl I liked in the leg. Until this day she probably still hates me. (And if you are reading this, you know who you are, and I am sorry again from the bottom of my heart. I hope your leg healed and your life got better.)

One night, this girl I really liked invited me to a party at a club. She told me not to bring certain friends because she didn't want no drama this night. I told her nothing would happen; everybody just wanna have fun. I knew it was a promise I couldn't keep, but I still gave it anyway. We got in the club, and the gang who the people I hang out with don't like is in there. She whispers in my ear, "Don't get in no shit tonight. For real," she said. I was like, "I'm not, I'm cool, I promise I got you, nothing is going to happen." I lied, unintentionally. We are about five deep: two of my homeboys, me, and it's her and her homegirl. They also knew another group of girls that would be in the club. The other guys are about ten to fifteen deep, maybe more. Out of nowhere, they started disrespecting us. Rapping the lyrics to the song coming through the speakers and putting middle fingers up and gang signs that disrespected the ones I was with. I felt they did that because they had strength in numbers. We weren't scared, and we responded. It went on for a little bit. Then eventually a fight broke out when one of my boys threw a drink over there and all hell broke loose. Security was doing what they could to break it up, separating us from trying to fight. Someone got hit with a bottle. It was chaos, as you can expect. The bouncers must have threw most of them out first. We eventually made our way out of the club. After them throwing everyone out, we were trying to get to the car. We were waiting for my girl's homegirl to get through the crowd and come outside. While we were waiting around, shots started ringing out. POW POW POW POW. Everybody that's outside started screaming and scattering. Before I could realize what was happening, I was hiding behind a car. I look not too far from where I was ducking at; I seen my girl got shot in the calf and she was screaming and crying. I went over there to her, trying to calm her down. I couldn't believe she got shot. Her getting shot I knew in some way was my fault. While I didn't pull the trigger, I know that bullet wasn't meant for her. I knew I made her a promise, and I didn't keep my word.

Three weeks went by and when we thought everything was cool, shit hit the fan. We were all at my boy's girl's house. She was cooking. They had a little studio in the house so some of the homies were over there rapping. It was good vibes. Then my boy asked me to go to the store to get some cigars. I didn't feel like driving at the time; I said, "No I ain't going to no store." He shot back at me, "You're a lazy-ass nigga." I just laughed, so he told his cousin to go. Maybe ten minutes after his cousin leaves, we hear a bunch of shots go off and a car speed off. We ran outside to see my boy's cousin lying in front of the car. At first you can tell he was trying to breathe, but it was hard for him. Then his chest just stopped going up and down.

If you take away the guns and the street beefs, the number of funerals I have had to go to … it goes from double digits to three. The sad part is, I got introduced to death so early that I've become numb to the pain. After seeing some of your friends in a casket, after a while it really can make you heartless. It leaves you with an empty feeling. When someone kills one of your people, it makes you want to kill two of theirs just so they can feel more pain. The issue with that is, then those people got people, so they want you to feel the same pain too. It's like a never-ending cycle. You are living in a nightmare you can't wake up from.

The streets are a cold place, I learned. You can be hanging with someone the whole time and you are thinking this is your boy because he is in your corner cheering for you. Really, the whole time he hates you are winning; he's jealous, and just waiting for that opportunity to stab you in the back. I learned the hard way; everyone is not your friend. The truth of it was that, chances are, on the streets, no one is your friend. Like the jungle, a hungry tiger will eat his own kids if he hungry enough. This shouldn't be life, but it's my reality; it's my nightmare from the bottom.

Chapter 7

Damaged Goods

One of the first lessons you learn, and possibly the toughest lesson you learn, is the streets don't got no loyalty. There ain't too many feelings worse than having someone around you thinking they are real, and they are actually the complete opposite. In the streets, you can't trust no one. Especially when there's money involved. Like Biggie said in the song "10 Crack Commandments"—"Your moms'll set that ass up, properly gassed-up, hooded, and masked-up, shit, for that fast buck. She be laying in the bushes to light that ass up."

Unfortunately, I learned this lesson the hard way and, luckily, I'm here writing this book. There are people I know that're no longer here because they trusted the wrong person. Someone they thought was their brother, their ride, or die homie.

The first time I was ever crossed I thought I was going to die. God was really on my side that night. It was a summer night and one of my homies I used to look at like a brother called my phone. "Yo! JD, you straight?" (Which meant, did I have any drugs for sale, or was I out?) I replied, "Yeah." I asked did he need me to pull up on him at his spot. He was like, "Nah, I'm somewhere different, so meet me." I said OKAY, he sent the address and I looked on the GPS. I really didn't know the area, but it was off the highway, and I was good with directions. I turned my music on, and I headed that way listening to music and talking on the phone. As I pulled up in the parking lot, I got this feeling in my gut that something isn't right, but I choose to ignore it. I pushed down the fear.

I pull up in the parking lot of the closed supermarket. I park near his car. He walked over to me and usually it's a bunch of jokes, but this time he was straight to the point. I should have known something was up because he was a little shaky and distant. He said to me when he walked up to me, "Did you bring what I asked you about? My cousin trying to shop for a new plug." I looked at his cousin with his hands in his pocket. I replied yes. I should have felt like something was going to happen, but I felt like I could trust this person. So, it was no need to have my guard up. I was also arrogant. I thought nobody would ever rob me.

I was known to put in work. At this point in my life, I was always ready to bust my gun. Boy, was I wrong. I learned none of that matters; anyone can be got. I learned when money is involved, don't trust no one. Only trust the one you see in the mirror.

I replied, "Yeah, I got so-and-so," as I reached in the back seat, under the passenger seat. My boy's cousin pulls out his pistol and someone jumped out the back of the car they were riding in holding an AK-47. I immediately threw my hands up and scream,

"What the fuck, bro?" The one with the pistol said, "Give me all that shit." They took my money, my drugs, the chains I was wearing, and my phone. All I could do is keep my hands up and plead not to shoot. All that kept going across my head is that I'm not dying right here, but if I did, I guess it would be my karma for all the robberies I went on. But I ain't never kill nobody. That was my first time I was on the other side of the gun of a robbery. The streets got no rules whatsoever. I was learning it was a tough lesson to learn. That lesson came with a price and, luckily, I didn't have to pray with my life.

I had friends that stole from me, but this was different, though; it was a new feeling. Even though it came with the game, it was a tough lesson to learn. When things like that happens it only makes your heart colder. Imagine a friend you hang out with often. If they fought, you fought. You all got money together. Someone you felt like you can trust all of a sudden robs you at gunpoint. How many emotions do you think you feel in that moment? Yeah, anger is at the forefront and, eventually, you learn to move different. If you're smart. Of course, you got to get revenge. It still doesn't stop the thought of what could have happen to you. I can say that it affects you for life. It's still hard to trust people after that. Not saying I completely stopped, but I started to slow down and watch my surroundings better. That story ended bad so many times for so many others. No matter how mad, no matter how big of a loss that was at the time, or even the beef that took place between me and him after. I had to be thankful I walked away with my life.

In Chapter 2, I said it took me seventeen years to find out what unconditional love is. I said that because that's when my oldest son Josiah Davon Reeves was born. He was born at five pounds, ten ounces. He was a small baby. I never loved anyone so much. This was my first blood relative that I knew. Everyone else was related to me by adoption or by the streets. I loved everything about this little soul. I took my son with me everywhere. I held him all the time. I knew I would do anything in my power to make sure he was good. That's exactly what I did. His birth didn't keep me out of the streets. Josiah's birth did save me a couple times from being in some pretty bad situations. Like one time when two of my homies came to get me to go with them to go do a couple burglaries. I didn't go and they got caught. One told on the other one. I will go into that story later in the book. I probably was one of the youngest out of the people I hung out with, but one of the most advanced. Trauma will do that to you. Like them child soldiers over in Africa. I was one of the first people in my circle to get a house and try to live the family man life. My first apartment I wasn't even old enough to lease by myself. I had to get my adopted mother to cosign for me. It didn't take much to convince her. She wanted me gone and all the trouble away from her house and I had a baby on the way. She didn't want none of that in her house. Moving on my own, I always made sure my homies were good and had a place to stay. No matter what.

I had two more kids with the same woman right after Josiah. I had Justin Jr. and Eriyanna. Josiah birthday is October 13, 2010.

Jr. birthday is September 23, 2011 and Eriyanna birthday is November 21, 2012. They were all back-to-back-to-back. Before Jr. came, I was still trying to find my way. I didn't know what I wanted out of life. I just wanted to survive. I knew I had to do more because I was going to be a dad of two boys now. I was working and selling weed. Six months before Jr. was born, I caught a petty drug case and had to go away for a couple months. After I got out, I slowed down in the streets for a little bit. I just worked and left the illegal activities alone. I went and finished my GED and enrolled in college for audio engineering at Full Sail University. It was like I was starting to get my shit together.

My mental health at this point in my life was more of me making it worse than trying to work on it and heal. I still had my mental health battles, but I put them on a back burner and became determined to do something more in life. I never even put thought into my mental health. I was too busy worrying about Jr.'s arrival. Jr.'s birth was special; it was the only birth I had someone close at the hospital with me, my best friend who was always like a brother, Latrell. Me and Latrell met my freshman year of high school. He was goofy to me at first, always telling jokes, so I didn't like him too much. Then after being around him for a while, I grow to love him, and we been friends ever since. Latrell had just moved back from Florida, when Jr. was born, so it was great having him there.

I was going to school online, but it was hard to keep up. I didn't like going to school online and I needed a hands-on experience. I wanted to get away at the same time. I tried to get into a college in Atlanta at the art institute. In order to go though, I would have had to do the summer course. Which would require me to pay the full fee for the course. I couldn't come up with the money. Let me rephrase that: it's not that I couldn't, I was only working at Walmart and making $8.15 per hour and getting paid every two weeks. It was almost impossible. I was always broke, and that week I didn't get paid was always a struggle week; I had no money. So, I said fuck it. Plus, I asked my adopted mother for the money. She didn't give it to me. That hurt me a little bit. Only because I knew she had it and I was seriously trying to better myself in life. It also made me realize nobody is not going to give me nothing. I got to go get it on my own. So, despite the attempt at the straight life, I went back to what I knew. I couldn't take it; I needed money and I knew how to get it.

Six months after Jr. was born, me and my girl at the time found out we were having a baby while we were at a close friend of mine's, Boo Gotti house. It's fucked-up because my boy Boo Gotti got shot and killed a month after we found out. Boo was twenty-five at the time and I even asked him to be godfather that night we found out we was having a baby. Eriyanna was going to be our third child and I was only about to turn twenty years old at the time. The good news of the new baby didn't last long, matched up to the tragedy.

Boo Gotti's death is a day I will never forget. Every detail and every feeling I felt that day will always be fresh on my mind like it was yesterday, no matter how much time pass by. It was April 20,

2012. At this point in my life, I was working and selling drugs, but mostly being a middleman. A middleman, for those that don't know, is not the one with the product but knew where to get it. When you get that product, you usually get it for a cheaper price, then you resell it a little higher than what you got it for. Sounds familiar? That's what a lot of businesses in America do. I was doing enough just to get by, so I didn't have to live check-to-check and could get my kids the things they wanted. I also was making decent money at the time; it was the most I ever made on a job.

I was working at a warehouse that Unc got me a job at. I will tell you more about who Unc is later in the chapter. I had just got off work and it was 3:00 in the afternoon. I had tickets to the Kevin Hart live standup What Now tour. The show was at 7:30. I really didn't have too much time to play around. I had talk to Boo the night before the show. I told him I would pull up when the show was over. I wanted to show him a song I was working on at the time. He told me to pull up and he cracked a joke about me messing up his game because he was trying to buy the tickets from me a couple weeks ago, when I first got them, and I didn't sell it to him. He told me to call him tomorrow when I leave the show. I was supposed to call him when I got off work, but my phone died when I was talking on the phone.

I didn't go home immediately. I pulled up on one of my homeboys from work. His house wasn't too far from the job. Plus, it was 4/20—that's National Weed Smokers' Day. It's like an unofficial holiday for weed smokers. We smoked a couple blunts and talked for a little bit before I went home. I was happy I knew I was going to have a good time at the Kevin Hart show. I went the last time he was in town in 2011 and I had a great time. I expected the same thing this time around.

I was living back at my adopted mama house at the time. I was evicted out my apartment that February. So, with nowhere to go I paid my adopted mother to let me, my girlfriend, and my children move in.

When I walked through the door after work, I went to the kitchen to make me something to eat because I was hungry after work and I was smoking too, so I had the munchies. My adopted mama was watching the news in the living room area, and I saw them mention something about Raymond Street with yellow tape. I couldn't hear what they were saying, and I really wasn't paying attention. I looked at the TV and seen they mentioned the street Boo Gotti lived on. I yelled out, "That's Boo street! I hope my nigga good." I didn't think much of it because in my mind I just knew my boy was good. With time moving closer to showtime, we started getting ready. We got the kids settled and left out for the arena. I saw Boo brother Amp call. I said to myself I would call him back after the show. I needed my battery so I could take pictures. I was going to Boo house, so I knew Amp would probably be over there or I would stop at his house; he lived around the corner from Boo.

I had a blast at the Kevin Hart Concert. It was hilarious and that's why Kevin Hart is one of my favorite comedians to this day.

Too bad the fun didn't last too long. I walked to the car talking about the funny jokes I just heard. Repeating them and still laughing. When I got in the car, I put my phone on the charger because it died halfway through the show. The first person I called when my phone powered on was Boo because I told him I was coming over after the show was over. It was weird because his phone was never really dead, especially this time of night. He never let his phone die; he even used to talk shit to me about that. After trying a couple of times, I called his brother phone. His girl at the time who is like a sister to me answered the phone. I said, "Yo! What's going on with Boo phone?" She got quiet and said, "Justin, you ain't hear what happen?" I could hear the pain in her voice. I became really concerned. I replied, "Nah, my phone been dead all day." She said, "Boo gone! Someone killed him!" I was not ready for that. I dropped my phone and froze. When I picked it back up, I repeated what she said, like maybe I didn't hear her right. She confirmed that's what I heard. I told her, "I'm on the way right now," and hung up the phone. Tears immediately fell from my face. I sped over to where his brother lived. I ran through red lights and didn't stop at the stop signs. Amp and Boo were blood brothers, so I knew he was taking it hard. I actually met Boo through Amp. Me and Boo connected off the music. Then friendship grew; he was a good person, he was genuine, he was kindhearted, and he was very talented. He was a real friend; he didn't deserve to go out like that. He was only twenty-five at the time.

When he got killed, it really fucked me up. He didn't deserve to go out like that. To be robbed by someone you know when your back was turned. That shit really hit me. He wasn't out here on no crazy shit, heavily involved in nothing crazy. My boy wasn't in any gang. He didn't even have any beef. Bro was just talented; he could have really made it in music. He was killed off pure hate and envy. The worst part is that no arrests have been made or any details even came out. Another one the streets claimed behind senseless violence. After that, for me, I wanted to get away. Away from the streets, away from life, away from everything; I needed to. On top of those feelings of wanting to escape. I was also angry the streets had several stories of what happened that day but nothing solid. I do know the love I had for him, the person I was then, I would have definitely got some revenge if we would have found out who had something to do with it.

Losing Boo was tough. The only thing kept me going was being a dad. I find purpose in that. When I'm at my lowest I always remember the promise and commitment I made to my children. One thing I told myself I would never do no matter how hard things get is I will never turn my back on my kids or let them go without. I always did whatever I had to do to make sure they always had what they need. I never needed no one to buy a pack of Pampers or even a pack of wipes. I don't care if I had to steal them out of the store. My pride wouldn't let me come up short. I always did what I felt was best and whatever it took. I survived by living any means necessary. I did some things I can't say I'm proud of, but I can stand on as a man. If I had to tie up the local drug dealer and take everything he was selling. It was just what I had to do. If I had to scam by cashing illegal checks, I did that. If I couldn't afford food or diapers and I had to go in a store and fill up the diaper bag, I did that. I was never going to let them feel that stomach pain when you are hungry and there's nothing to eat. It was a feeling I was familiar with and a feeling I was not going to let them experience. I was never going to let my babies go without. Especially when shit hit the fan. My kids are the only reason I didn't lose it after Boo Gotti got killed. I couldn't eat for days. I didn't even show up to work for a couple days. I went from being sad to angry to sad again. After my friend was killed, three weeks later, I caught four assault charges and some other drug-related charges. Now I was homeless, living in a hotel with the kids and their mother.

How had I end up in that predicament? I got into a big brawl with my adopted mother's neighbors. It was a few days before Mother's Day. I was cleaning out my car and playing music on a Friday afternoon. I was not bothering no one. When the neighbor came over to me and immediately snapped at me about the music being too loud. At this point in my life, I'm twenty years old and I got my third child on the way. I just lost a close friend of mine, so I wasn't up for the bullshit. I felt I was grown, and truth be told, I hated to be disrespected, especially when I'm not disrespecting you. So, when she snapped at me, I was not trying to hear nothing she was saying. I immediately shot back at her "I ain't turning shit down if you gonna talk to me like that!" She threatened to turn the music down herself. I just gave a daring look and responded, "You not gonna touch my car." So, she rightfully did what any woman would do in that situation and go get her husband. Not like that phased me; I have faced much worse people.

Her husband came outside with their son and another guy yelling at me. My adopted mother and kids' mother also ran outside after they heard all the commotion. The husband was furious as he was walking towards me talking shit. To be honest, I knew he stood no chance. Not saying I'm the baddest man in the world; I just knew this is what I loved. Violence is something I knew all too well. I was still standing in my adopted mother's driveway unbothered because I know I can fight. Win, lose, or draw, but I'm never fearing another man.

That's what happens and develops over the years for some of us. You just build a mindset to always be on go and ready for whatever comes your way. It's a warrior's mindset. You add that to the anger I had built up inside of me. I knew I was going to fuck him up bad. My mother stepped in front me as he is yelling and pointing and coming towards me. I tell him, "If you come any closer to me, I'm going to fuck you up." Ignoring the warnings and not knowing what I was dealing with and dealt with in the past. He still got in my face with my mother standing right there. I got fed up quick and pushed her arm down from holding me back and I immediately punched him two or three times and he fell. Usually, I would get on top and beat his face in, until someone stopped me.

Then I saw the son and like a shark on his next victim I still wanted more blood. So, I ran up to him and just started swinging on him. He didn't want to fight and tried to run but I tripped him and started punching him. Then the other guy who was with them tried to grab me and we started fighting. He got a good hit in, but not good enough. I was going to do him bad, but my kids' mother ran in between us and grabbed me. They ran back to their house to call the police. I ran to my phone to call my homies. I felt like I got jumped even if I was handling myself well and won those fights. In my mind it wasn't over. The thought of them trying to do that to me had me ready to escalate the situation even more.

Bubba and all my homies pulled up instantly; they were in the neighborhood right next to mine. They got there fast. What was so crazy to me, and I never seen before, was how quick the police came. I don't know what they told the 9-1-1 operator, but six police cars raced into where we were at. They jumped out, guns drawn. Yelling for each person to get in their yard. My mother was walking up to one of the officers. The officer yelled at her, "Go back to your yard!" She responded back, "I'm on their side." Feeling confused after what I just heard, I just watched a few of the officers go and talk to them first. I knew I was going to jail at that very moment. How did I know? I knew they was going to believe whatever they said. My reputation and run-ins with the law got me once again.

Most of the cops and detectives who patrolled that area knew who I was and who I rolled with and what we did. They just couldn't always prove it or build a case. One of the officers who was standing over by me, as I was sitting in my truck drinking a bottle of water, he asked me what happened. I told him they started it. As I was going into details, the officers that was talking to the neighbors walked over to me and told me to stand up and he handcuffed me. They searched my car and found some weed and took me to jail. I gave my kids' mother some money out my pocket to get a hotel room, because they informed her we wouldn't be able to stay there. Luckily it was a Friday, so I had just gotten paid. I didn't care about going to jail.

I thought I was going to get out of jail the next day after bond court. I had the money to bail out. I went to bond court that next morning. It was a lot of us. I don't know if you ever been arrested, so if not, I will tell you the process about how they do it at this jail. Every jail and every state operate a little different. You get to the jail, the police hand you over to the intake officers. They process you, ask you questions about your health and mental health, and make you see a nurse. You get to use the phone and call your family. They dress you out after and put you in a unit before you go to bond court to classify you; whether you got a misdemeanor or felony, you go to two different parts of the jail. If you don't bond out in three to four days, they move you to the part of the jail you have to go to.

In the morning it was quite a few of us that had to go to bond court. When they finally got to me, the judge was reading off my charges. Then he asked each person was they scared for their life.

The wife said no she's not, the husband said no he's not, the other person didn't show up and the family answered for him and said no. When the judge got to my mother and asked her, at first, she got quiet. Then he asked her again. "Are you scared for your life, ma'am?" She replied, "Yes!" My heart sank to the bottom of my stomach. If I had to compare that feeling to anything, I would compare it to being punched in the stomach by Mike Tyson in his prime with all his strength. All the air left my lungs. I couldn't show that emotion though because I was in jail and I'm damn sure not about to let no one see me weak.

The only mother I knew since I was young turned her back on me and on top of that was lying on me just to get rid of me for her neighbors. I didn't hear nothing else after that. I went back to the unit and waited for my bond to post. I called my kids' mother and she posted it. As I was waiting for my name to get called, a C.O. brings me a paper and tell me there is a hold on me and I couldn't get out. I had a warrant in another county. For driving under suspension and simple possession of marijuana. For some lucky reason they didn't come pick me up and I got out of jail a few days later. When I got out, I had to go straight to work; my shift already started and I didn't even get to celebrate Mother's Day because I was in jail.

Me, my kids, and their mother started living out of a hotel room where we stayed for the next fifteen months of my life. I was paying $300 a week because my pride would not let me live with no one else; I didn't want no roommates. I didn't want to crash at nobody's house. I kept faith, I did whatever I had to do to survive and made sure we were good. Like I said earlier in this chapter, I worked, I hustled, I scammed, and a few times I even robbed a few people. They were caught in the crossfires of my life and it wasn't personal. I just know my kids will never tell me they were hungry and there not be something for them to eat. They were never going to go without. I made a pledge to myself. I knew what it was like to go without.

I bust my ass to give my kids everything I never had, and I always start by giving them the love I always wanted. The affection and even the time I always wish I could have got from a parent. I always felt if I had that love, that genuine love, I would have turned out much better than I did. I eventually stopped doing robberies and burglaries completely when my unc got on me and called me out for how I was living.

Let me give you a little history on me and Unc relationship. I met Unc when I was fourteen years old. Me and some of my boys was cutting through his yard to get to my neighborhood, and I said let me ask can we cut through his yard, because he was in his back yard messing with his dogs. When I asked him, he cracked a joke and said, "Don't y'all little badass kids steal shit." We laughed, but he let us cut through. He looked at me and said, "You're different; you got respect. You can cut through anytime." What made our bond close was one day me and my adopted father was fighting (not the time he stabbed me). This was one of the many fights we had. I can't really remember what we were fighting about, but I went to Unc house and asked him can I just do my homework over here. I told him the situation. He let me chill. After that, he took me under his wing and looked out for me. He told me "I'm not trying to be your father, but I got you." I couldn't look at anyone as a father figure, so I called him the next closest thing which was Unc. He is like an uncle I never had, always giving me knowledge and debating with me about sports, music, and life. I learned a lot from him. Fast-forward back to 2012, the conversation we had that kind of got me in line. Notice I did say 'kind of.' It at least got me to stop robbing people.

I called him one day to help me move to a different hotel. I had robbed someone, and I knew there was a chance they might come trying to get back at me. I only got $1,500, but I didn't want the retaliation to come near my kids. I called him and said, "Unc, I need you quick; it's an emergency. I'll tell you when you get here." Unc was from the streets too, and even did time back in the day, ten years, to be exact, so he knew what time it was when I called. He came, he helped me, and I explained the situation to him. He looked me dead in my eyes when we were done and said to me, "Nephew, that ain't the way. You can't keep robbing Peter to pay Paul; that shit is going to catch up to you. The day it does, you don't want them kids with you." He told me, "I love you, but you on your own; don't call me on no bullshit like this again. It comes a time when you got to be a man and figure out what's more important to you." Before he left, he gave me a couple hundred dollars and drove off. I was never mad at him for saying that because he was always there for me, and deep down, I knew he was right. He did something to me that day, though.

He put a fire in me. For the most part, my intentions were always pure and good. I was just so damaged, so it took a lot to see the good. The good things waiting for me in life, the good that was in me or the good that was around me. I eventually got out of the hotel and found a small two-bedroom apartment in the basement of a boarding house. It was nowhere nice, but it was a step up from the hotel room and was cheaper; $160 a week. That was some type of progress. It was nowhere near where I wanted to be in life. I still had a long way to go just to get back to the bottom.

My life is proof that the saying, 'once you're at the bottom there is no place to go but up' is bullshit; you can definitely go lower and make things worse. It all depends on your mindset. If you keep a negative mindset, you're going to only make things worse, and negative is going to keep happening to you. I had to want more. I had to think positive. I had to see the light even when there was none; I would just imagine it. So, I kept grinding and trying to climb up. One thing is for certain though, to know me is to love me, and to love me you got to be someone special, because I'm damaged goods.

Chapter 8

The Post-Trauma

My whole existence, I've always felt a disconnect to life. Like I was missing something. In reality, I really was. I was missing the love of my mother. Not saying that my path would have been any better or easier. At least when I went through it, I could have gotten a hug and for her to lift me up and encourage me. I would just imagine her telling me, "Things will get better, son. I love you, son." With her absence, I never really learned how to love or even to accept it. Most of my life lessons came from learning things the hard way or from the streets. I hit the wall so many times. I guess that's why my head was so hard.

The fact I wouldn't let nobody actually love me made it hard on the women I was dealing with. The fact I didn't even know who I was and still trying to find my place in life, made it damn near impossible for anyone to love me. I really felt like I needed love and someone to care for me. For the people who grew up with a parent and lost their parent later in life as an adult: could you imagine feeling that pain you feel your whole life? That emptiness inside affected a lot of the decisions I made in my life.

My trust has always been fucked-up. I always feel like someone is plotting on me or up to no good. Being betrayed or having close people do cruel things to you will have that effect on you. When it came to my relationships, I loved, but I was reserved. It was hard to let anyone get close to me. I thought getting married would fill that void and complete me. That only made a temporary fix. The marriage didn't last too long. I know now you can't hold onto a person because you fear being alone and you don't want to face your own demons.

Me and my kids' mother got married in 2014 and was separated and divorced by 2016. Now I can say I wasn't ready for that. I came to the decision to get married while I was in jail on a ninety-day plea deal for the assaults and drug charges. I got married for all the wrong reasons. I only got married because I felt it was the right thing to do. The idea of having someone there for me for the rest of my life wasn't a bad idea, especially when I was used to being and feeling alone. I didn't care if it was the right person for me or not; I just wanted someone there. I was released in March of 2014. We got married, and in August of 2014 we were splitting up. She ended up moving out and moving across town with her friend and I ended up going back to all I know. The Streets.

I was back hustling and scamming. Taking trips going out of town with my cousin. Doing anything to get a quick dollar and a come-up. Me and my cousin ended up getting a house we turned into a trap house. For the readers that don't know what a trap house is, it's a drug house. Let me tell you, things took off fast.

Before you know it, within two weeks of moving in our spot, we were making over $600 a day. On a side of town we weren't from. It created a lot of competition and haters. Me and my cousin ended up falling out over a disagreement. I felt like he was moving shady, and he left me for dead. He ended up making a move with a friend he grew up with and leaving me to fend for myself. He told me he couldn't get no more weed from his out-of-town connect, but some strange reason the spot with his friend had weed. I knew it was bullshit and it caused us to fall out for a little bit. I was in the jungle alone now.

The only thing about that is that you throw a tiger in the jungle … he's gonna eat. That's exactly what I did. While hustling with my cousin, I made a few connections on my own. I was also saving some of the money I was making. I didn't have a car at the time, so I really didn't go nowhere. I wasn't buying clothes to stay fresh at this time. I was just letting my money stack up. After we fell out and decided we wouldn't deal with each other no more, I went and bought my own weed. Even though the prices were way higher, I had to show him I could make it without him. I was selling weed and wasn't making nowhere near the money I was making before, but I was making something. I couldn't get as much either, as I usually had; the prices was too high.

When me and my cousin fell out, it hurt me big. Not emotionally or nothing like that. It hurt my pockets big time. The person the weed was coming from was my cousin's connect which was out of town, like I said. I never met him; I just know he had really great prices. With no out-of-town connect on weed at the time, I had to shop local. The ones who was my competition, I was taking all their customers; I needed them now, but it was impossible to find someone in my city to supply me with the same numbers I was getting out of town. They weren't going to do that; most people don't have it in them to watch someone else win and be happy for them. They didn't care if I could have moved the weed faster and it would have help both of us. The image of being "that guy" means more to some people. The satisfaction of seeing me fall after blowing up fast probably was even more of a reason for them to not help me. I got tired of the headache and aggravation, and I just went to selling crack. It seemed like the right step. I was back down, and my back was against the wall. I wanted that quick money. The feeling that fast money gives makes the dark days feel a whole lot brighter. It doesn't fix shit in the long run. The faster the money, the faster you spend it … the faster you lose it.

Plus I was away from my family; I was away from the one thing that meant the most to me. Which are my kids. I was lost without them. My younger two kids were living with their grandmother two hours away and the older one was living with their mother across town. I had no way of going to see them.

I had no car until my mentor, who later became a big brother to me, gave me one. Michael Breedlove. I knew him from the juvenile center I was at when I was fifteen. He worked there even after being released. I always kept in contact with him. He ended up giving me a car for free. Not only did he give it to me, he taught me how to drive a stick shift. He told me he got a new car and didn't want to just sell it. He said if I can learn how to drive it in one day, I can have it, because that's all the time he had to teach me. Of course, I learned. I was determined; I needed that car. I knew getting that car would fix a lot of my problems. Till this day, I'm forever grateful to him and I would give him one of my kidneys if he needed one. Not only because he gave me the car, but he has been there for me on so many occasions when I needed him.

That car came in handy, and it saved my life in many ways. It added to my profitability because it made me mobile. Things got hot real fast as the police began watching the house and the motel on the corner we would also hustle at. Too many people were hanging out there and too much was happening. Parties, fights, and a couple of shootings. The landlord ended up serving an eviction to get me out, which was a blessing in disguise. I had time to leave. The court date was in two weeks, and I still had thirty days after that if I wanted. Deep down, I wanted my family, mostly my kids back.

Like I said, being a dad gave me purpose. Without them, I had none. I was just getting through the days. Before the court date for the eviction, I ended up taking the money I got off a scam and saved up from hustling. I found a house and I went and got my family back together. I moved to another side of town in the middle of the night. Two weeks later they raided the motel and fifteen people was indicted. I was really close to a few of them. Luckily, I wasn't there, or my name never came up in any paperwork. Come to find out, the whole time they had an informant in the motel. The crazy thing about that is that I never served the informant. The one time we came in contact, he asked me did I have anything to serve him. I didn't serve him because I was in a rush to go spend time with my kids. They gave my boy fifteen years behind that. Just another instance of where my kids saved my life.

I've been to too many funerals and seen too many of my guys in and out of jail. A deep part of me always wanted to break the cycle. Break it for me, break it for them, and break it for our kids. Hell, break it for our parents, too. I can't act like I've never tried to escape the streets. I worked and did the family thing and got one foot out the streets, but I could never get the other foot out, so I usually ended up right back in. I guess no matter how much I try to elevate, a part of me is comfortable in the environment because I know how to survive.

I wasn't the type to sit around and wait for someone to hand me anything. I was always the type to go get it. To me, working all these hours and waiting on my money never sat right with me. Getting paid the bare minimum was not something I was into. Working until I'm sixty-five just to retire, then take trips. I was not feeling that. I always felt like I was better than this. I never felt I was above or better than anyone. I just knew I had way more potential, and I was supposed to be doing something bigger. I knew there had to be a bigger purpose for me. I didn't suffer all this pain just to punch a clock until I get old and retire or die, and

I definitely didn't survive all that shit just to get shot or end up rotting in jail. I also knew the streets weren't the life I wanted, but it's the only life I knew.

The thing that made me want way more was traveling and seeing the country. I started taking trips to Denver, Colorado for weed because I got tired of paying those high prices. I knew I could get it cheaper, so I did. I started jumping on planes and sometimes even driving across the country handling business by myself, or I would go with a friend. Most people wouldn't have taken that risk. Me, I looked it as high risk equals high reward. I was determined and nothing was gonna stop me. Doing that successful for some time made me know I could do anything at that point. It was like, "Look how far I came. I turned myself into a plug. I went from being the guy who always had to find it, to being the guy who everyone came to get it from." I had leveled up. I knew if I could make it this far, whatever I wanted in life I could have.

My problem is just seeing myself more than just another person from the streets. When this has been your reality for so long, sometimes you start believing that this is all life has to offer. For me, just to clarify, I saw the world as a loveless, trustless black hole that ended one of a few ways. The thing that keeps me going and keeps my hope up is my children. I never want them to have to go through this. I can't say that enough. I never want to raise a street nigga. As a single dad now with three boys, I know I got to do something to show them better. Dealing with the aftereffects of everything left me with a battle on the inside. A battle of me versus me. A battle of who I was versus who I'm trying to become. For their sakes, I'm going to win that battle, and I'm going to make my past distant from my future.

Chapter 9

A Battle Within

As you read in the previous chapters, I lost a lot in these streets. Spilled blood, shed tears, and learned a lot of lessons. I learned lessons that Harvard or any college couldn't teach. I learned how to follow codes. How to adapt in any situation, how to live with honor, and most importantly, how to take nothing and make something. Unfortunately, to get these lessons I had to endure a lot of pain. A lot of times things are this way because everybody around you is damaged. Most people coming up, all they received was pain. So, as they get older, they go from receiving pain to inflicting pain on people. Have you ever watched a situation go from zero to one hundred in a matter of seconds? How does an accidental bump on the shoulder result in the loss of life and the person who died was only trying to break up the issue? How do two people who just called each other "brother" try to kill one another? I'll tell you, sometimes pride gets in the way. Someone can't accept the fact of taking a loss. So, they decide to cause pain and take things to the extreme. In some places, it's so crazy that they turned killing into a sport. Who can rack up the bodies. Most people I talk to ask, "Can things ever change?"

I would say in my lifetime, probably not. You got years and years of trauma and pain passed down from generation to generation to generation. Most of the time, the next generation has to find their own way. Once you are in that world it becomes your reality. As you can see, for me at certain times in my life it was just about making it to the next day and if I was able to survive it. My mentality was. "I'll figure it out when I get to it." It was just about surviving. Now as a single dad with my three boys, it's about living. It's about maximizing my potential and not being afraid of the process along the journey. Accepting it's okay to elevate and it's ok to not look over my shoulder. Telling myself, "Justin, you are a dad now; you don't have be out here in these streets." Having the proper mentality is what get you through. A lot of it. It's hard to shake because you never really heal; you just learn to cope. For some people, they will do anything to escape the reality of how fucked-up life can be.

Some people turn to drugs; others turn to alcohol. Some try to make money to make it out or just to be the man. If you're going to be in a fucked-up environment, might as well be that guy, right? You don't have a family? Most join gangs and create that family. Then some people have no fucking clue, they just there like a bush or a tree or something static. Just lost, living day to day, accepting whatever life gives them. Then some find a purpose. A purpose in their life that drives them. Once that happens is when the battle within starts inside you. The battle I fight day to day.

My mentality got me this far, but how much further could it really take me? Eventually, I got to elevate past that. We all do, little by little. For every one person that tries to elevate and break free, that's a future generation that doesn't have to suffer. For me, I began wanting more than this, than the streets. I know the end result is the same for people either one of two ways: Jail or Death. We all roll the dice and gamble hoping we make it out before one of those two things happen. Where do I go from here? My only option is to elevate. I have been at the bottom for so long. This type of change doesn't just happen; you have to want it and you have to make it happen. This battle, I'm not sure you ever win, but I'm damn sure going to give my all in fighting it and helping other people fight it.

Yes, sometimes I get survivor's remorse. I left a lot of friends out there. But now, it's time to stop feeling sorry for still being here and actually start to embrace it. To be really honest, I wasn't supposed to make it past twenty-one; hell, I even had a person tell me I won't make it to my eighteenth birthday. I'm twenty-eight now, and hopefully still have a lot of life left to live. I'm nowhere near where I want to be, but I came such a long way.

I may still not be able to sleep because of the nightmares. I may never sit with my back to an exit. I may still be cautious when cars speed off or pull up beside me funny at lights. I still may get jittery when someone turns the corner with their hand in their pocket and the hood covering their face. I may always look over my shoulder and feel like someone wants to kill me. That isn't going to change for a while. The only thing I can do is continue to elevate my mind. Understanding and knowing my position. I'm a king on the board and not a pawn and understanding the only thing that separates the two is the way they move and the purpose they serve. If you don't play chess, they both can only move one space at a time. The king, however, can move any direction he likes, and the point of the game is to capture the king. The pawn can only move one space forward at a time, unless it's capturing someone; then it can move one space diagonal. But the pawn can be sacrificed and replaced. I say all that to say to you, the reader, "Always have a plan and know who you are and your position." For now, as I suffer with the trauma I dealt with from the streets, I truly hope me and every single person that's fighting that battle within gets through it all. I hope you overcome the darkness and that good in you prevails as you elevate to the life you deserve.

My children always gave me a purpose. When I couldn't find one, they helped me look within myself and find mine.

Being a single dad to three boys isn't easy, but it's worth every struggle. As I grow into my purpose, I want to show my kids something different. I do not want them to repeat the cycle and go through the things I went through in life. Kids tend to do as they see, not as they are told. Let's be honest; they may not get to be as fortunate as I was to slip through the cracks. So, it's up to me to show them a different way. They are my advantage to the battle I fight on the inside simply because I know I owe it to them to give them my all and live out my purpose. Plus I want to be their role model. I don't want them having to look outside for one. Sure, they could look on TV or turn on the radio, but none of those people are their father. I want my kids to look at me as a role model and to show them you can be successful no matter what you go through. I can't tell no one how to find their balance or how to seek your purpose. I can only tell you how I find mine. I dug deep. I believed and always wanted more. Am I all the way balanced? No. As you know, parenting itself has many challenges and twice as many for a single parent. Plus all the other battles I fight within. Such as depression, being traumatized from the streets, and elevating myself. One thing I do know: if you keep searching for it, you will find your balance and your purpose. The best way by doing that is to start looking within.

Chapter 10

JD Final Thoughts

Let me start by saying, if you made it to this final chapter, thank you from the bottom of my heart. Thank you for being a part of this journey and I hope you continue on the journey with me as I release more books and dive into other ventures. It took me a long time to get to this point. My book is finally complete. This is the first time I started something and finished it all the way through. No matter what, this is one of my biggest accomplishments and no one can take it away from me. The first time I ever wanted to write a book I was fifteen years old. Of course, then I didn't get it done and a few other times I wanted to do it I didn't get it done. I'll write a few pages and I would stop. I created stories with fictional characters, then other times I would write about my life. I even started writing a book of poems before. All would usually end up the same: incomplete.

After a lot of failures and cutting out a lot of the distractions, I was able to overcome each obstacle and finish the book. I realized I didn't need a happy ending. Hell, my happy ending is I'm still alive and I didn't let none of the shit I been through stop me. This is not even half of the things I have done or been through. I just chose the most relevant parts of my life to get the message across.

I didn't do this to prove I'm a gangsta or to glorify the negativity. Truth be told, the most gangsta thing I have ever done was to step up and be a father to my children. My path was my path and I live with no regrets. Truth be told, I wouldn't trade my life for anyone's. The things I been through made me who I am today. This book is purely to motivate the ones like me who is struggling with whatever they are battling. If it's an addiction, if it's depression, if it's some type of mental disorder, if it's to get out the streets, or even just want to level up and you don't believe in yourself. You can look at me, you can read these stories, and say, "He made it through; I can do it too." You can do whatever you want in life. If you believe and put the work in. The fact I didn't have parents or received the proper love. I didn't use that as an excuse to not love my kids, to be an absent parent, or even be a shitty person who treats people like crap because they are miserable inside. I chose to do and be the complete opposite. I give my kids the love I wish I had and give them the love I never received. I chose not to make excuses for myself. I chose to not get comfortable, and instead, always push myself for more. I chose to not let my situation define who I am. Yeah, I had to do a lot of fucked-up things and a lot of fucked-up things happened to me. I never felt sorry for myself. I just tried to find a solution and I always did what I had to do. Even if it wasn't right. I don't regret anything I have been through, nor am I ashamed of the things I have done or been through. I'm not afraid to fail because I know that's where the true lessons are. Yeah, I suffer deep inside. Yeah, I want to throw the towel in sometimes. Yeah, sometimes it's even hard to find a purpose. I live with a lot of pain. It's bad to the point I barely sleep at night. I just learned to cope. I chose to get back on my feet instead of staying down every time life knocked me down. I found out not giving up is actually the hardest thing to do, and by not giving up, I'm stronger than I think. Do I have all the answers or big degrees? No. I just have a lot of experience on survival. As I fight this battle, I'm not even sure that I'm winning. I hope you can take something from me and learn. I know it sounds cliché, but you really can make life what you want. When I was on the block, in the trap, or on a job, I always knew I could do better than this and my purpose got to be bigger than this.

To all my guys and ladies in the streets that suffer from post-traumatic streets disorder: I say, live in the moment; appreciate the good moments. Yeah, they might be few and far apart, but cherish them and always look back on them and always try to make more good moments. I do understand that all pain isn't temporary and some of it last a lifetime. You still got to live; it's okay to be a survivor. Just find purpose in whatever you do. If it wasn't for me becoming a single dad, I would definitely still be out there. I had no choice but to find mine. So just find your purpose; you got this. You made it this far; there ain't no reason you can't make it any further. In closing, my story is nowhere near the worst story, as there are people who went through way more traumatic things than me. The thing that separates me from most, though, is the fact I stayed pure and true to who I was through it all. I defined my situation and didn't let it define me, like I said a few paragraphs ago. Until the next book, thank you and I love all my supporters and readers. This was from my heart to your heart.

Peace and Thank You.